SONIA SOTOMAYOR

SONIA SOTOMAYOR

A Biography

Meg Greene

GREENWOOD BIOGRAPHIES

AN IMPRINT OF ABC-CLIO, LLC
Santa Barbara, California • Denver, Colorado • Oxford, England

Copyright 2012 by ABC-CLIO, LLC

Library of Congress Cataloging-in-Publication Data

Greene, Meg.
  Sonia Sotomayor : a biography / Meg Greene.
     p. cm. — (Greenwood biographies)
  Includes bibliographical references and index.
  ISBN 978-0-313-39841-4 (hardcopy : alk. paper) — ISBN 978-0-313-39842-1
(ebook) 1. Sotomayor, Sonia, 1954– 2. Judges—United States—
Biography. 3. Hispanic American judges—Biography. I. Title.
  KF8745.S67G74   2012
  347.73'2634—dc23 [B]   2011053373

ISBN: 978-0-313-39841-4
EISBN: 978-0-313-39842-1

16 15 14 13 12   1 2 3 4 5

This book is also available on the World Wide Web as an eBook.
Visit www.abc-clio.com for details.

Greenwood
An Imprint of ABC-CLIO, LLC

ABC-CLIO, LLC
130 Cremona Drive, P.O. Box 1911
Santa Barbara, California 93116-1911

This book is printed on acid-free paper ∞

Manufactured in the United States of America

CONTENTS

SERIES FOREWORD

In response to school and library needs, ABC-CLIO publishes this distinguished series of full-length biographies specifically for student use. Prepared by field experts and professionals, these engaging biographies are tailored for students who need challenging yet accessible biographies. Ideal for school assignments and student research, the length, format, and subject areas are designed to meet educators' requirements and students' interests.

ABC-CLIO offers an extensive selection of biographies spanning all curriculum-related subject areas including social studies, the sciences, literature and the arts, history and politics, and popular culture, covering public figures and famous personalities from all time periods and backgrounds, both historic and contemporary, who have made an impact on American and/or world culture. The subjects of these biographies were chosen based on comprehensive feedback from librarians and educators. Consideration was given to both curriculum relevance and inherent interest. Readers will find a wide array of subject choices from fascinating entertainers like Miley Cyrus and Lady Gaga to inspiring leaders like John F. Kennedy and Nelson Mandela, from the greatest athletes of our time like Michael Jordan and Lance Armstrong to the most amazing success stories of our day like J. K. Rowling and Oprah.

   While the emphasis is on fact, not glorification, the books are meant to be fun to read. Each volume provides in-depth information about the subject's life from birth through childhood, the teen years, and adulthood. A thorough account relates family background and education, traces personal and professional influences, and explores struggles, accomplishments, and contributions. A timeline highlights the most significant life events against an historical perspective. Bibliographies supplement the reference value of each volume.

INTRODUCTION

In October 2009, if one were to knock at the door leading to the conference chambers of the Supreme Court, according to tradition, the door would be opened by the court's newest member, Sonia Sotomayor. This particular Supreme Court justice is more well known for her salsa dancing, karaoke singing, and affinity for the New York Yankees baseball team. She is a life-long resident of the Bronx in New York City. Sotomayor appears to be following the lead of her predecessor Ruth Bader Ginsburg and has been seen wearing a white lace collar under her stern black judge's robe. What most people do not realize is that this justice, the third woman and the first Hispanic ever to ascend to the highest bench in the land, also brings more federal judicial experience to the court than any other Supreme Court justice of the last century.

Sonia Sotomayor has been painted as a left-leaning judge who, if one believes the conservative elements in the nation, will push the Supreme Court further to the left than the court has seen in decades. Other political pundits and legal analysts have deemed Sotomayor as being more centrist and that instead of embracing a strong political agenda, she will rule on cases much as she has since she first became a judge: according to the law. She will also demand of the lawyers

*Justice Sonia Sotomayor, 2009, at
the Supreme Court in Washington.
(AP Photo/Charles Dharapak)*

nothing less than the most polished arguments that they can present, just as she did as a young prosecutor.

Even though Sotomayor may be the court's newest member, she conducts herself as if she has been on that bench for a lot longer. In her first appearance on the Supreme Court's opening day, Sotomayor took an active role in hearing oral arguments. She asked as many questions and made as many comments as Chief Justice John G. Roberts Jr. As the *Washington Post* reported, the only clue that Sotomayor was the new judge on the block was that she forgot to turn her microphone on before asking questions. This is in sharp contrast to other justices like David H. Souter, who spoke little during his first year on the bench, or Justice Clarence Thomas, who has not asked any questions during the last three years.

Sotomayor's presence as one of two women on the court is important too. Both current Justice Ruth Bader Ginsburg and retired Justice Sandra Day O'Connor have stated how important it is to have more than one woman on the Supreme Court bench. Not only does it give the American public a better view of the court, it makes it more difficult for the male justices to ignore the woman's point of view when discussing courtroom cases, when there are more women in the room.

Sotomayor's presence has also brought up comparisons to Thurgood Marshall, who sat on the court from 1967 to 1991. Marshall, the court's first African American justice, exerted a profound influence over the court, and was known for not only sharing his legal expertise but his life experiences as an African American man growing up in the shadow of racial prejudice. If anything, Marshall pushed the Supreme Court not only to respond to the most persuasive legal arguments of the court but also to a moral compass. Both of these qualities have also been applied to Sotomayor as well.

Sotomayor knows a thing or two about stereotypes and has spent a great deal of her time in battling them as a woman and as a Hispanic. And while she welcomes the opportunity to serve as a role model for these two groups, she also cautions that she comes to the Supreme Court not to serve a specific group of people, but to serve all and to interpret the law in the best way possible. She has said that she will be guided by two key pieces of advice given to her by two former Supreme Court justices. From David Souter, Sotomayor learned that the key to an amiable relationship with other members of the court is to remember that every justice, no matter his or her background, or political leanings, or personal beliefs, should act in good faith when he or she makes his or her decisions.

The second piece of advice came from Justice John Paul Stevens, who retired in 2008. In talking with Stevens, Sotomayor expressed her doubt at her abilities in achieving the kind of quality legal thought that Stevens was known for. Stevens told her, "Sonia, I wasn't born a justice. . . . I've had many, many years. You have all the skills to be a great justice, but you have to develop them and grow into them."[1]

It is still too early to tell what history will say about Sonia Sotomayor and her time on the Supreme Court. But by every indication, she has shown that she intends to be a viable and vocal voice on the bench and it is not inconceivable that Sotomayor may have a hand in forging potentially new directions in American thought and law. She brings with her a tremendous energy and intelligence and it is hard to imagine her not leaving some kind of imprint that will also shape the Supreme Court in years to come.

With the addition of the Supreme Court's newest member, Justice Sonia Sotomayor, top row, right, the high court sits for a new group photograph, September 29, 2009, at the Supreme Court in Washington, D.C. Seated, from left are Associate Justice Anthony M. Kennedy, Associate Justice John Paul Stevens, Chief Justice John G. Roberts, Associate Justice Antonin Scalia, and Associate Justice Clarence Thomas. Standing, from left are Associate Justice Samuel Alito Jr., Associate Justice Ruth Bader Ginsburg, Associate Justice Stephen Breyer, and Associate Justice Sonia Sotomayor. (AP Photo/Charles Dharapak)

Much has been made of Sotomayor's rise to the highest court in the land. Her story mirrors many American immigrants: the humble surroundings, the importance of education, the will and determination to succeed, sometimes at overwhelming odds. These very elements can inspire or become clichés. In Sotomayor's case, her life is clearly the former, for it gives meaning and hope to others that the American dream is still alive, well, and enduring.

NOTE

1. Adam Liptak, "Sotomayor Reflects on First Years on Court," *New York Times,* January 31, 2011, http://www.nytimes.com/2011/02/01/us/politics/01sotomayor.htm.

TIMELINE: EVENTS IN THE LIFE OF SONIA SOTOMAYOR

June 25, 1954   Sonia Maria Sotomayor is born in Bronx, New York.

1962   Sotomayor diagnosed with diabetes.

1963   Sotomayor's father, Juan Sotomayor, dies.

1972   Attends Princeton University.

1976   Graduates from Princeton, marries, and begins law school at Yale.

1979   Graduates from Yale and begins working at New York District Attorney's office.

1980–1992   Board Member of the Puerto Rican Legal Defense and Education Fund.

1983   Tarzan murder case, Sotomayor divorces.

1984   Sotomayor joins the firm of Pavia & Harcourt in New York City.

1986   Fendi Crush at Tavern-on-the Green, New York City.

1987   Appointed to the New York State Mortgage Agency.

1988   Appointed to the New York City Campaign Finance Board.

1991   Nominated to the bench of the U.S. District Court for the Southern District of New York by George H. W. Bush.

1992 Confirmed to the U.S. District Court for the Southern District of New York.

1995 In *Silverman v. Major League Baseball Player Relations
Committee*, issues an injunction against the owners of
major league baseball teams, ending lockout.

1997 Nominated for the U.S. Court of Appeals for the
Second Circuit by President Bill Clinton.

1998 Appointed to the U.S. Court of Appeals for the Second Circuit.

2009 In *Ricci v. DeStefano*, rules against New Haven, Connecticut white and Hispanic firefighters over exam
results.

2009 Nominated and appointed to a seat on the U.S. Supreme Court.

Chapter 1

LIVING THE DREAM

In 1999, Judge Sonia Sotomayor faced the graduating class of Lehman College, located in the Bronx, New York. She told the class that she had deliberated for some time about what to tell them. "I decided to tell you a story," she began, "the story of my mother's life. . . . It is . . . a story of what hope, hard work, education and dedication to make a better life can achieve." It is also a story of the courage, vision, and perseverance that one woman showed as she tried to improve not only her fortunes but also those of her family. To understand the daughter, we must first look to the mother.[1]

THE GIRL FROM LAJAS

The city of Lajas, Puerto Rico, is in the region known as Valle de Lajas (Lajas Valley) and Las Lomas de Sudoeste (the Southwestern Hills), located in the southwestern part of the island. The land extends to a vast plain situated between two hills: Las Lomos de Santa Marta (the Hills of Santa Marta) to the north and Sierra Bermeja (the Brownish-red Mountains), which runs to the south. To the north also is the city of San German; to the south are the blue waters of the Caribbean. To the east are the cities of Guánica and Sabana Grande; and to the west is Cabo Rojot. Lajas covers approximately 60 square miles and is composed of 11 barrios, or neighborhoods.[2]

The story of Lajas is rich in myth and legend. The origins of the city date from the mid-18th century when it was a small, poor village. Near the village, however, was a spring that flowed from a rock. Replenished by the heavy rains and protected by trees that obscured the waters, it seemed inexhaustible. The village took its name from smooth, flat limestone rocks surrounding the spring. The locals called these stone slabs *lajas*.[3]

There is also a more romantic account to explain how the city was founded. According to local legend, many years ago, a farmer walking toward his home stopped to rest in front of a Higüero tree, a kind of fig tree found in many parts of Central and South America. When the farmer gazed at the trunk of the tree, he was startled to see the image of the Virgin of the Candelaria, a Black Madonna carrying the Christ Child in one hand and a green candle in the other. Days later, the farmer returned to the tree, where to his surprise the image remained. Only after the second viewing did he decide to tell his neighbors in the village of San Germán of what he had seen. When the other villagers accompanied him to the tree, the image had vanished. Dismayed, the villagers discussed what the image could mean and why the farmer had seen it. In the end, they convinced themselves that the Virgin had made a request of them, asking that a chapel be built on a nearby hill. The villagers honored the request, built the chapel, and, in time, several families moved to the area. And that, according to legend, is how the village of Lajas came to be.[4]

A NEW MASTER

Celina Baez was born in 1927 in a neighborhood called Barrio Sabana Yeguas, known as Cañitas, a rural area to the south of the town center. The landscape was dominated by sugarcane fields, which once served as fodder for cattle. By the time of Celina's birth, the sugarcane had been transformed from cattle food to a cash crop, thanks in part to the takeover of Puerto Rico by the United States after its victory in the Spanish-American War of 1898.[5]

For more than three decades, sugarcane was Puerto Rico's largest export, accounting for almost 60 percent of the island's foreign trade. The majority of sugarcane was grown by four large American corporations that bought or leased land from local farmers, and earned millions of dollars a year. The promise of a fertile land and a workforce ripe for exploitation translated into millions of American investment dollars to Puerto Rico. To aid American business, the American government built public works projects such as roads for industry and schools for the native children.[6]

Despite the influx of American dollars, the lives of many Puerto Ricans did not improve. The semifeudal society, united by language, religion, and culture, had been replaced by a vast and unsettling abyss between Puerto Ricans and their new American bosses. As one observer noted, "In the future there will be prosperity . . . but there will be no fatherland. And if there is, it will belong to Americans and their children and their grandchildren. Within half a century, it will be a disgrace to bear a Spanish surname."[7]

THE IRELAND OF THE AMERICAS

If, as another writer declared, the "American flag found Porto Rico [sic] penniless and content," the Americans could not have done more to disrupt the familiar rhythms of life by trying to mold the tiny country into the image of their own society. Large, modern factories soon dominated the countryside. In them, native Puerto Ricans, many of whom had lost their land to the big American corporations, toiled in misery, earning as little as 12 cents a day or approximately $3.49 per week.[8]

The poverty and resulting inequality were devastating to the tiny nation. The Americans built schools, yet less than 40 percent of the citizens could read. Of the island's 77 districts, only 2 had doctors. The death rate from tuberculosis, malaria, and hookworm was astronomical. Where once even the poorest farmer might have a chicken or two, a pig, and a small plot of land, now he could not feed himself, to say nothing of his family. Life for many who dwelled in the Puerto Rican countryside had become unmitigated misery. No longer seen as one of the "most interesting and incompetent nationalities in the world,"

Puerto Ricans were now hopelessly caught in the tight grip of American government and business.[9]

Even as the sugar economy was booming at the end of the 19th century, other sectors of the economy were flagging. The cultivation of coffee, once the mainstay of the Puerto Rican economy, suffered a series of disasters beginning with the outbreak of war in 1898. Workers who for years had toiled on the coffee plantations took the opportunity of the Spanish-American War to turn on their employers. Coffee haciendas were burned and ransacked and some plantation owners killed. To make matters worse, the harvested coffee did poorly in the market, due to a surplus. As a result, prices fell, and many Puerto Rican coffee growers were financially ruined. As if things could not get any worse, the following year, 1899, one of the island's most devastating hurricanes, San Ciriaco, destroyed many of the coffee plantations. Homeless and jobless, workers streamed into the cities and sugar-producing regions looking for work, further stressing an already struggling economy.[10]

GROWING UP IN THE BARRIO

Many members of Celina Baez's family, including her cousins, worked in the sugarcane fields or transported the raw sugar to the local mill where it would be crushed and refined. The work was backbreaking and unprofitable. To the residents of Bario Sabab Yeguas, the sugarcane fields might have symbolized poverty and desperation. The bright yellow Roman Catholic Church in the town square, by contrast, gave them a measure of hope, no matter how small.[11]

Celina Baez's childhood reflected her surroundings. Frequent pregnancies and unremitting poverty had left her mother, Pancha Tora, weak and ill—so ill, in fact, that after Celina's birth, she never left her bed. Though she lived nearly 20 more years, she continued to be in poor health and finally died in 1946. Celina's father, Agustin Baez, perhaps overwhelmed by his wife's illness and the prospect of raising five young children without much help from her, abandoned the family not long after Celina was born. By this time, the older children had to take care of themselves as well as their younger siblings. Two of Celina's older siblings, Mayo and Aurora, took primary responsibility for her, though they were not much older than she was.[12]

Celina did attend school, though there was no money to buy pencils or books. Instead, she tried hard to remember what she had read in books and heard her teacher say. She returned home each day and spoke her lessons to the trees, repeating as best she could all that she learned. Over time, she named the trees after her classmates, and, pretending to be the teacher, recited each day's lessons to her students. Her pointer was a stick that she found. As her daughter later recounted, these moments offered Celina a brief respite before she returned to the house to begin her chores.[13]

The Baez children were not completely alone, however. Their paternal grandmother, Juana Baez, tried to help with childrearing, as did an uncle who lived nearby. When Celina's elder sister married, it was decided that Celina would move with Aurora and her husband to the town of San German. The move, however, did little to lessen the oppression of poverty that continued to plague the family. By this time, one of Celina's brothers, Mayo, had also married and moved to Mayaguez, where he purchased a farm on which he grew vegetables and bananas. Many times, Mayo's fruits and vegetables went not to market but to help out the family when food was scarce.[14]

THE PROMISE OF A NEW BEGINNING

Celina seemed destined for a life of hard work and poverty. But in 1944 an opportunity arose that promised her a chance to lead another kind of life. The United States was in the midst of World War II against Germany in Europe and Japan in the Pacific. To support the war effort, men and women from all walks of life joined the armed services. Even though Puerto Rico was only a U.S. territory, Puerto Ricans supported the cause too: 22,000 men joined the ranks.[15]

The Women's Army Corps (WACs) came to Puerto Rico to recruit young women for the Transportation Corps and the Medical Department. The Transportation Corps alone employed 5,000 WACs in offices and military installations at several major port cities, including Boston, New York City, Hampton Roads, Virginia, Charleston, South Carolina, New Orleans, Seattle, Los Angeles, and San Francisco. It was from these areas that American troops boarded ships and planes for overseas duty.[16]

Because there was such a shortage of civilian personnel to handle the traffic, the WACs had been entrusted with the job. The WACs made little effort to recruit minorities until late in the war. But because there were not enough people to handle the duties at the embarkation centers and, despite concerns over language barriers, the call went out to look for recruits in Puerto Rico. In April 1944, a four-woman recruiting team arrived on the island. The team, which consisted of one officer and three recruits, distributed applications. The response was overwhelming: more than 1,500 women showed up to fill 200 positions. Among them was the 17-year-old Celina Baez, who had seen the recruiting advertisement in a San German newspaper.[17]

Identifying suitable candidates was difficult; many women were rejected because they could not pass the aptitude test. Others had problems with English. A large number withdrew because their parents had strenuous objections at the possibility of a young, single woman leaving home and taking a job with the United States Army. Celina almost lost her chance to come to the United States—after doing well on her aptitude test, she faced the objections of her sisters who hated the idea of their youngest sibling going far away to an unfamiliar and potentially dangerous place where she might get into trouble.[18]

Celina eventually prevailed, and on October 6, 1944, she was among the first 51 recruits disembarking at Miami, Florida, for the journey to Fort Oglethorpe, Georgia, to begin WAC training. Celina was in heady company; compared with her own meager educational background, of the 100 women who were recruited in Puerto Rico, almost 40 percent had college degrees and were, prior to the war, working as teachers or business professionals. Despite their level of education, many of the women spoke little or no English. As a result, the group was kept intact instead of being integrated into other WAC units. Their lack of English also worked against them in that they did not receive assignments commensurate with their intellectual capabilities.[19]

AMERICA

When she arrived at Fort Oglethorpe, Celina was immediately plunged into a busy and structured world. According to the WAC manual, the intensive training was to instruct recruits to how to "salute, how to march, how to look like a soldier, how to handle a gas mask, and how to make a bed the Army way." In addition, women who had specialties, that is, office skills, nursing skills, and so on, would be encouraged to use them. Those women, like Celina, who had no special training or knowledge, were to learn specialties. With an added incentive of $50 a month, many young women found the grueling training worth the effort.[20]

By the time of Celina's arrival, Fort Oglethorpe was serving as one of five WAC training centers: 1,000 women a week entered the four-week basic training course. Once they had completed their training, the women were sent to their posts, which might be in the United States or abroad. And so it was for the next month, Celina learned how to live the army way: marching, doing calisthenics, undertaking office and equipment training, cleaning, and performing kitchen duty. In the meantime, she met other women who came from all over the United States.[21]

Celina was determined to overcome her shortcomings in the language and culture of America and to meet the expectations of her new employer, the United States Army. Sonia Sotomayor commented many years later on the overwhelming culture shock her mother must have felt: being a young woman, working for the U.S. military with a grammar-school education. Even the simple task of answering the telephone was a challenge for someone who lacked the rudiments of English or who was unfamiliar with the telecommunications technology. According to Celina, the first time she picked up a telephone, she heard a voice requesting to speak to her sergeant. Celina went looking for him to give him the message. When her sergeant reached the phone, he was dismayed to hear only a dial tone. Celina had hung up the phone believing that's what she was supposed to do. It was a mistake she did not repeat again.[22]

A NEW LIFE—NEW YORK

After completing her training, Celina and the Puerto Rican unit were assigned to the Port of Embarkation in New York City. The women were among the approximately 100,000 Puerto Ricans involved in the war effort. The Port of New York encompasses more than 1,200 square miles, with New York Harbor alone sprawling for approximately 430 square miles. New York had 11 ports that included the waterfront areas of Manhattan, Brooklyn, Queens, the Bronx, and Staten Island as well as New Jersey from Perth Amboy to Elizabeth, Bayonne, Newark, Jersey City, Hoboken, and Weehawken. This entire area encompassed approximately 650 miles. The port also included 1,800 docks, piers, and wharves of varying sizes and types. Of this number, 750 were classified as active; 200 of these areas could dock 425 ships at the same time. Six hundred additional vessels were at anchor in the harbor.[23]

During World War II, the harbor was partitioned into 600 individual ship anchorages that could accommodate ocean-bound vessels that awaited docking or were loaded and were waiting to disembark. On a peak day in March 1943, 543 merchant ships lay at anchor in New York Harbor, putting the harbor close to maximum capacity. Estimates suggest that between the Japanese attack on Pearl Harbor in December 1941 and V-J (Victory in Japan) Day in August 1945, more than 3 million troops and their equipment and over 63 million tons of supplies and materials were shipped overseas through the Port of New York.[24]

Not everyone believed that the WACs were the best choice to staff the busy port. As one military historian wrote, "Early pessimists feared that the ports of embarkation were not the place for WACs, who would undoubtedly be invalided by the rough physical work or seduced by the transient combat troops." But the group had few problems dealing with their new assignment. In addition, many of the soldiers were entranced by the accents of the women, and were more often than not happy to cooperate with their requests.[25]

The women, known as the Transportation WACs, carried out a variety of duties. Many were assigned to postal battalions where they processed the V-mail letters. A V-mail letter, which was shorthand for the term "Victory Mail," was a special postal process used during World War II to send and receive letters from overseas. V-mails involved transferring the original letter to special film to reduce space. The letter was also censored to remove any information that could potentially be used by the enemy. When the letter arrived at its destination, it was printed back on paper for the recipient to read. At the New York office where Celina was stationed, the women opened the letters, checked to make sure that they were correctly formatted in order to be either transferred to film or printed back on paper, looked for rips and tears, and then sent them on to the commercial company that photographed them. The women also checked incoming letters; with these, the women operated machines that put each letter in an envelope. It was monotonous work, requiring 24-hour duties consisting of several shifts.[26]

Other duties that the women undertook included working at the piers in different capacities. At first, WACs were in charge of processing female civilian personnel, nurses, and other WACs bound for overseas duty or who were returning to the United States. Soon the women were put to work processing all types of personnel—men and women—who were embarking from or arriving at the port. These WAC checkers as they were called labored on the piers and ships, where they processed not only outgoing military and civilian personnel, but also an estimated 800,000 items of war material for overseas forces.[27]

A typical day might include keeping records of the types of guns, the proper ammunition for each, and the type to be issued to each man according to his destination. But the WACs' duty did not end until they actually handed the gun to the soldier. The WACs were also employed in more creative ways, such as the all-WAC orchestras that traveled out on small boats to meet the ships and welcome the returning soldiers back home. When the ships docked, WAC teams met the soldiers and carried out roll call and helped the men through routine checking. Once this was completed, another group of WACs escorted the soldiers to the proper train to carry them to their next destination. Overall, the women had few problems completing their assignments. As one report noted, "Directions given [by WACs] to troops debarking were cheerfully obeyed for the men 'just wanted to hear them talk.'" More than a hundred Red Cross women were so impressed with the way the WACs handled their jobs that they wrote to a commanding general: "It is our unanimous opinion that we have never been in an area where everything functioned more smoothly. There has been none of the confusion or discomfort which we had come to consider a normal part of the embarkation process."[28]

A WAVE OF PIONEERS

Celina Baez came to New York at the end of what was the first great wave of migration of Puerto Ricans, which dated to the early 19th century, when a number of well-to-do Puerto Ricans moved to Manhattan and its environs. Many of these early arrivals were men and women who had been exiled by the Spanish for their political beliefs, including the idea of a Puerto Rico free from Spanish rule. Staying in their homeland would have meant imprisonment; banishment at least allowed many to keep their money and possessions, which the Spanish did not confiscate. With the outbreak of the Spanish-American War in 1898, Puerto Rican migration came to a standstill.

Not until the first decades of the 20th century did Puerto Ricans again begin to arrive in New York in significant numbers. During the first great wave, which occurred between 1900 and 1945, the *pioneros* established themselves in New York City. These early pioneers made their homes in the Atlantic Street area of Brooklyn, El Barrio in East Harlem, and a few other sections of Manhattan such as the Lower East Side, the Upper West Side, Chelsea, and the Lincoln Center area. Others settled in the neighborhoods of the South Bronx.[29]

In 1917, with American entry into World War I, the United States Congress passed the Jones Act, which granted Puerto Ricans American citizenship. This meant that Puerto Ricans no longer needed a passport to travel to the United States. With the Puerto Rican economy suffering from hurricanes and the damaging effects of American business on the land, many Puerto Rican families migrated to the United States, in particular to New York City. For many, the prospect of a four-to-five day trip cramped in a steamship was worth the misery for a chance to improve their lot.

Like earlier immigrant groups who settled in New York, such as the Irish and the Italians, the Puerto Ricans faced many hardships and much discrimination. Because many could not speak English and few had technical skills, finding a job was difficult. The jobs that were available tended to be in factories where wages were low, conditions poor, and job security nonexistent. The new arrivals also faced hostility from other immigrant groups; in 1926, Italians attacked Puerto Ricans in East Harlem, a neighborhood where both groups resided.

Despite these problems, Puerto Ricans continued to come to New York City in greater numbers. In 1920, there were 7,634 Puerto Ricans living in the city; by 1930, 45,000 had come in search of better opportunities. By this time, too, the group had established its own institutions including stores, social clubs, and churches, which made New

York even more attractive for incoming migrants. On the eve of World War II, more than 69,000 Puerto Ricans called New York home.

By the time of American entry into the war in 1941, job opportunities for Puerto Ricans had improved greatly. For many men, the military beckoned; Puerto Ricans were fiercely patriotic and devoted to the Allied cause. With the large numbers of American men fighting, there was a desperate need for manpower to fill jobs. Puerto Ricans, both male and female, found themselves employed in factories and shipyards producing both consumer goods and war materials. It was against this backdrop that Celina Baez came to New York City in 1944.

WAR'S END

Even after the war ended in August 1945, Celina and her WAC unit were kept busy at the New York City port processing the thousands of soldiers returning from military duty. During her time in New York, Celina met a young factory worker by the name of Juan Luis Sotomayor. Born in 1921, Sotomayor had come to New York City with his family from the Santurce district of San Juan, the capital of Puerto Rico. Originally, Sotomayor had worked as an auto mechanic, but he eventually left Santurce to come to New York City in search of a better job. Armed only with a third-grade education and with no knowledge of English, he nevertheless found employment at a tool-and-die factory, a job that not only paid well, but also taught Juan a valuable skill.[30]

Not long after Celina was discharged from the army, the couple wed. Together the two set out to make a new home and a new life for themselves in the city, settling in the South Bronx. Even though Celina could have found a job in which she need not speak English, she chose to get her high school equivalency certificate, which would allow her a wider range of job opportunities, while also improving her mastery of the English language. She enrolled in the GED program at James Monroe High School, located at 1300 Boynton Avenue and E 172nd Street in the Soundview neighborhood of the Bronx.[31]

Because the test was given only in English, Celina had to work to get her language skills to the required level. The exam consisted of several sections, including social studies, science, reading, writing, and mathematics. Celina's determination to master the exam was tremendous;

her hard work paid off and she passed the day-long exam on her first try. Now armed with her GED, Celina made the rounds searching for a job. She soon found a position as a telephone operator at Prospect Hospital in the Bronx, where she earned a reputation as hardworking and tireless employee. She was encouraged to continue her studies and pursue a practical nurse's license. But as much as Celina wished to continue her education, there were other matters to consider, such as starting a family. For the time being, education would wait.[32]

NOTES

1. Lisa Lucas and David Saltonstall, "Sonia Sotomayor's Mother Tells News: I Overcame Odds to Raise U.S. Supreme Court Pick," *New York Daily News*, May 27, 2009, http://articles.nydailynews.com/2009–05–27/news/17922654_1_celina-sotomayor-supreme-court-sonia-sotomayor.

2. "Lajas, Puerto Rico," http://www.lajaspr.com/engHistoriaLlama.htm.

3. Ibid.

4. Ibid.

5. Cèsar Ayala, "The Decline of the Plantation Economy and the Puerto Rican Migration of the 1950s," *Lationo Studies Journal* 7, no. 1 (winter 1996), pp. 63–65.

6. Earl Parker Hanson, *Transformation: The Story of Modern Puerto Rico*, New York: Simon & Schuster, 1955, p. 38.

7. *La Democracia*, "We Are Becoming Americanized," in *The Puerto Ricans: A Documentary History*, ed. Kal Wagenheim and Olga Jimenez de Wagenheim, New York: Markus Wiener Publishers, 1994, pp. 110–11.

8. Hanson, *Transformation*, p. 38; Luis Muñoz Marín, "The Sad Case of Porto Rico," in *The Puerto Ricans: A Documentary History*, ed. Kal Wagenheim and Olga Jimenez de Wagenheim, New York: Markus Wiener Publishers, 1994, pp. 154–55.

9. Muñoz Marín, "The Sad Case of Porto Rico," pp. 154–55.

10. Fernando Pico, "Let Puerto Rico Decide," *America* 178, no. 19 (May 30, 1998): 3.

11. Antonia Felix, *Sonia Sotomayor: The True American Dream*, New York: Berkeley Publishing Group, 2010, pp. 4–5.

12. Ibid.

13. "Induction Proceedings for Judge Sonia Sotomayor, November 6, 1998," United States Court House, 500 Pearl Street, New York, NY.

14. Felix, *Sonia Sotomayor*, p. 6.

15. Ibid., p. 7.

16. Ibid., pp. 7–8.

17. Ibid., p. 7.

18. Ibid., pp. 7–8.

19. Ibid., pp. 8–9.

20. *WAC Handbook 1944*, Women Veterans Historical Collection, University of North Carolina-Greensboro, http://library.uncg.edu/dp/wv/results28.aspx?i=4708&s=2.

21. Felix, *Sonia Sotomayor*, p. 9.

22. Ibid.; "Induction Proceedings for Judge Sonia Sotomayor, November 6, 1998."

23. Joseph F. Meany Jr., "Port in a Storm: The Port of New York in World War II," New York State Museum, http://www.nysm.nysed.gov/research_collections/research/history/hisportofnewyork.html.

24. Ibid.

25. Felix, *Sonia Sotomayor*, pp. 9–10; Mattie Treadwell, *The Women's Army Corps*, Washington, D.C.: Center of Military History, 1991, http://www.history.army.mil/books/wwii/wac/ch18.htm#b6.

26. Treadwell, *The Women's Army Corps*.

27. Ibid.

28. Ibid.

29. Clara E. Rodriguez, "Puerto Ricans: Immigrants and Migrants: A Historical Perspective," AmericansAll, A National Education Program, n.d., http://www.americansall.com/PDFs/02-americans-all/9.9.pdf.

30. Felix, *Sonia Sotomayor*, pp. 9, 11–12.

31. Ibid., pp. 9, 14–15.

32. Ibid.

Chapter 2

DAUGHTER OF THE BRONX

During her confirmation hearings for the Supreme Court, Sonia Sotomayor remarked, "my mother is so humble and so unassuming that she does not perceive herself as a special person in any sense, and she speaks about the burdens in her life in fragments and only sparingly. A close friend of mine once remarked, however, that the more interesting part of my life is really the story of my mother's life." By the 1950s, Celina Baez Sotomayor's life seemed to be on track. She was married, living and working in New York City, and dreaming of the opportunities that awaited her, her husband, and her future children. America's bounty seemed endless, and Celina, having had a taste of what the American dream promised, wanted more.

THE GREAT MIGRATION

Celina and Juan Sotomayor's story was being played out by the thousands of immigrants to the United States. By the early 1950s, the Sotomayors were part of the growing number of Puerto Ricans who had settled in New York City as part of what was known as the "Great Migration."

Sonia Sotomayor with her mother, Celina Sotomayor, in 2009. (AP Photo/J. Scott Applewhite, pool)

This period, which lasted from approximately 1950 to 1960, saw an estimated 470,000 Puerto Ricans come to the United States.[1]

This mass exodus from Puerto Rico was the result of several factors. Beginning in the 1930s, the agricultural economy declined. Exports such as sugar, coffee, and tobacco dropped precipitously. Coupled with this was an increase in the island's industrialization that began during World War II, when state-owned industries tried providing goods that the armed services needed but could not receive if the Germans imposed a naval blockade between the island and the United States.[2]

In 1948, Puerto Ricans elected their first governor, Luis Muñoz Marín, who had run on a platform of economic reform and improved relations between the United States and Puerto Rico. Marín believed that the key to improved relations was to develop Puerto Rico's industries. If manufacturing could be bolstered, Marín believed that the country's economic fortunes would take a turn for the better, and bring additional investment from the United States. As a result, the government launched an industrialization program known as Operation Bootstrap, which focused primarily on inviting American companies to invest on the island. To further entice the American companies, the Puerto Rican government offered incentives such as tax exemptions and help in building new factories. In return, it was hoped that the Americans would provide jobs to the locals. Marín and his supporters believed that both the United States and Puerto Rico would benefit from this exchange. As it was later described, Operation Bootstrap would provide jobs, step up industrial opportunities for outside investors, and allow the country to export finished products to the United States.[3]

Unfortunately, there was a downside to the program. With less focus on the agricultural economy, many rural workers found themselves without jobs. They now fled to the cities where they swelled the workforce by competing for the low-paying factory jobs. With such a large labor pool and fewer opportunities for work, many Puerto Ricans decided to leave for the United States, where there were far more jobs, albeit also comparatively low-paying ones. With the lure of cheaper airfares making travel more affordable, approximately 21,000 Puerto Ricans journeyed to the United States every year, gambling that they would find a better life in a new land.[4]

The greatest influx of Puerto Ricans came to New York City where Puerto Rican communities exploded across the Harlem River into the South Bronx and into sections of Brooklyn, such as Williamsburg and Sunset Park. Home for the majority of immigrants was the dilapidated inner-city neighborhoods where once earlier immigrant groups, such as the Italians and Jews, had lived. In time, Puerto Ricans became the second largest minority in New York City, after African Americans, and the second largest Hispanic population in the United States, after Mexicans.[5]

The majority of new arrivals were young males with few skills, little education, and almost no knowledge of English. Many found work in low-paying jobs such as light manufacturing, domestic service, and seasonal farming labor. Their reception, much like that of the immigrants who came before them, was often hostile, and many Puerto Ricans found themselves excluded from better-paying jobs, good housing, and good schools due to discrimination. It was against this backdrop that Juan and Celina Sotomayor settled in and began raising a family.

SOUNDVIEW

After their marriage, the Sotomayors moved to Soundview, a neighborhood located in the south central section of the Bronx. The neighborhood's boundaries were set by the Cross-Bronx Expressway to the north, White Plains Road to the east, Lacombe Avenue to the south, and the Bronx River to the west. Until the 1940s, the neighborhood remained comparatively undeveloped, with most of the dwellings consisting of multiunit row houses and tenements. Many of the units had been constructed near the El Westchester Avenue and along major streets such as Soundview Avenue, which made it attractive for workers commuting to and from the city.[6]

The first significant public housing development, Clason Point Gardens, was constructed in 1941. A number of low- and high-rise public housing apartment buildings followed in short order. One of these, the Bronxdale Houses, which, like many others was built by the New York City Housing Authority, became home to the Sotomayors. Bronxdale also was one of many new housing developments built as part of New York City's urban renewal program, which hoped to move families out of the slums and into new apartment buildings. The development, begun in the 1950s, consisted of 28, 7-story red brick buildings that contained 1,496 apartments located on almost 31 acres of well-tended and landscaped grounds. At its peak, the development was home to almost 3,500 people. For the planners and builders of Bronxdale these towers in the park offered the promise of a brighter future.[7]

During the 1950s and early 1960s, the Bronxdale Houses were respectable residences built for mostly lower middle- and middle-class families; approximately 10 percent of the development's residents were on welfare. Rents averaged approximately $51 a month and provided for many families an affordable home in a good neighborhood. The emphasis was on families at the Bronxdale; if an applicant was not working, was a single parent, or had a criminal record, his or her application was refused. Living at the Bronxdale Houses was nothing short of magical: "Here was a paradise," said Ricardo Velez, who was among the earliest tenants when he moved to his apartment in 1956. "It was beautiful."[8]

The grounds at the Bronxdale were carefully maintained: residents were ticketed if they walked on the grass. Children needed to be watchful, for neighbors acted as surrogate parents to make sure children behaved themselves. Neighbors looked out for each other; leaving bicycles and baby carriages downstairs was not a problem as people respected each other's belongings. For many families, such as the Sotomayors, moving to the Bronxdale was the first step to living the American dream; the residents even identified themselves as "Bronxdalians."[9]

During this period, the couple welcomed their first child, Sonia Maria, born on June 25, 1954. Not long afterward, Celina returned to her studies, hoping to earn her Licensed Practical Nurse (LPN) certificate. When Sonia was three, the family moved to Building 28 in the Bronxdale development. Although she was only a toddler, the family's move to the new apartment was one of Sotomayor's earliest memories:

> It had just been freshly painted and there were lights everywhere and the floor was clean. It was the cleanest apartment I had ever seen in my three years of living. And the memory was so overwhelming of walking into this pristine environment and realizing that this was going to be our new home. It overwhelmed me. And then I did what any child's going to do. I took my tricycle . . . and pedaled it into my bedroom. And as I did that I put a scratch on the wall. And I was absolutely heartbroken that I had marred this environment. I thought my mother would kill me and I hid under the bed.[10]

In 1957, the family welcomed its newest member: a baby boy, named Juan Luis after his father. By this time, Celina had passed her LPN exams and was employed at Prospect Hospital, where she proved to be a highly efficient and respected employee. For Celina, the avenue to advancement was in education. As her daughter recalled, "My mom believed that education was the key to everything in the world. If you became educated you could do whatever you wanted and accomplish whatever dreams you had."[11]

A BRONXDALIAN CHILDHOOD

Growing up in the Bronxdale development provided many happy memories for Sonia Sotomayor. The housing development was filled with families who encompassed a veritable mosaic of countries and cultures, though more than half of those residing in the apartments were Puerto Rican. There were also a large number of African Americans, Italian, Irish, and Jewish families. Days were spent playing with other children at the housing development's playgrounds. When not working, Celina visited with neighbors, chatting through the open doors of the apartments as women cooked, cleaned, and tended their children. Spanish was still the primary language of the house as Sotomayor's father never mastered English. When Celina and Juan were at work, a neighbor and close friend looked after the children. For Sotomayor, those early years at the Bronxdale were filled with many happy moments. "We had the run of the projects," Sotomayor wrote many years later, "We had freedom."[12]

If the week belonged to neighbors and friends, the weekends were reserved for family. Every weekend cousins, aunts, and uncles dropped in at the home of Juan's mother, Mercedes Ortega, where the family played dominoes and where the meals included plenty of traditional Puerto Rican dishes. Sometimes the grown-ups listened to music and danced in the living room, while the children played *loteria*, a version of bingo, placing chickpeas on their cards as their grandmother called out the numbers. Summer outings might be spent at Orchard Beach, known as the Riviera of New York, in the northeast Bronx, where the picnic lunch might include sandwiches, *pernil*, and *arroz con gandules*. Other weekends might be spent watching a baseball game at Yankee Stadium with her father, brother, and other relatives.[13]

But these family get-togethers involved much more than spending time with relatives. The experiences were an integral part of what forged Sotomayor's ethnic identity. At a speech given in 2001, Sotomayor described what the essence of these experiences was for her:

> For me, a very special part of my being Latina is the mucho platos de arroz, gandules y pernil—rice, beans and pork—that I have eaten at countless family holidays and special events. My Latina identity also includes, because of my particularly adventurous taste buds, morcilla,—pig intestines, patitas de cerdo con garbanzo— pigs' feet with beans, and la lengua y orejas de cuchifrito, pigs' tongue and ears. . . . Part of my Latina identity is the sound of . . the heart wrenching Spanish love songs that we enjoy. It is the

memory of Saturday afternoon at the movies with my aunt and cousins watching Cantinflas, who is not Puerto Rican, but who was an iconic Spanish comedian on par with Abbot and Costello of my generation. My Latina soul was nourished as I visited and played at my grandmother's house with my cousins and extended family. They were my friends as I grew up.[14]

Even though both of Sotomayor's parents worked, money was tight. Although as children she and her brother did not have everything they wanted, Sotomayor believes that her family life was rich in spirit. As she said later, "I never perceived myself as a poor child."[15]

A THREAT UNCOVERED

By many accounts, as a child Sotomayor was quiet and even withdrawn and listless. But then she began noticing things that did not seem right. First, she was thirsty all the time; no matter how much water she drank, she never felt satisfied. Then she began wetting her bed. "I was ashamed," she later said in a June 2011 speech to a number of diabetic children and their parents. Then, one Sunday morning, Sotomayor fainted at church. She was rushed to the hospital where the doctors decided tests needed to be done. A lab technician sat her down in a big chair and assured her the needle in his hand would not hurt her. But upon seeing the needle, Sotomayor thought otherwise. "I kept watching this big needle coming to my arm," she later recalled, "and I looked at him and I said, 'Oh, it's going to hurt.'"[16]

She hopped off the chair, ran out of the room and out of the hospital with the hospital staff in pursuit. She hid underneath a parked car in the hospital parking lot. When the staff finally found her, they took her back to the lab and drew the blood. "I was screaming so much I didn't feel the needle," she later recalled. As if the experience had not been frightening enough, there was more bad news: Sotomayor was diagnosed with type 1 diabetes.[17]

Type I diabetes interferes with the ability of the pancreas to manufacture insulin. Insulin enables the cells to process glucose (sugar), which provides energy for the body. The news hit her parents particularly hard, and for Sotomayor it marked the first time she saw her mother cry. Even though the doctor told her diabetes wasn't so bad, Sotomayor thought, "If it isn't so bad, why is my mommy crying?"[18]

With the diagnosis confirmed, Sotomayor had to learn how to live with her disease. Having a nurse for a mother helped in many ways. Sotomayor and her mother tested her blood sugar using razor blades instead of finger pricks. There was no soda pop, only the bad-tasting no-calorie drinks that contained no sugar. In an era before disposable needles, Sotomayor woke up early and boiled water to sterilize the syringes that she needed to inject insulin. She was so small that she had to drag a chair over to the stove to reach the burners. Eventually though, Sotomayor said, the acts became routine and her personality changed for the better. Having a chronic disease taught her discipline. "That discipline helped me . . . in every aspect of my life," she later said.[19]

A GREAT LOSS

The Sotomayor family had settled into a quiet routine by 1961. Visitors to the home were struck by the closeness of the family and the warmth extended toward friends. With Sotomayor's diabetes under control, she emerged from her withdrawn listlessness to become a happy child, fully engaged in her world and her family.

A year after Sotomayor's diagnosis, tragedy struck the family. Juan Sotomayor was standing in the kitchen of the family's apartment when he fell to the floor, clutching his chest. He was rushed to the hospital; by the next morning he was dead of a heart attack. He was only 44. He had suffered from heart problems for years, yet his death was completely unexpected. Like his wife, Juan Sotomayor believed in the American dream and was confident that his children would go on to achieve even greater things because they had the opportunity to do so. As one cousin later recalled, Juan Sotomayor would often say to his daughter, "*Algun dia, usted va a ir a la luna* (Someday you're going to go up to the moon.)" After her husband's death, Celina Sotomayor moved her family to smaller quarters in Apartment 2F, Building 24 of the Bronxdale Houses. She worked six days a week at the hospital to provide for her children. Sonia and Juan shared a bedroom and life soon settled again into a quiet routine. Celina ran an ordered household and the children, when not studying, helped with the chores. Every Sunday, the three would make their way to St. Anthanasious Roman Catholic Church on Bruckner Boulevard and Tiffany Street to attend the 10 o'clock mass.[20]

DISCOVERING NEW WORLDS

After her father's death, Sonia retreated into the world of books. Although she had friends, Sonia loved to read. Among her favorite books were the popular Nancy Drew mysteries that chronicled the adventures of a girl detective. The series was a long-standing rite of passage for many American girls. Sonia and her friends often visited the local library where they checked out the Nancy Drew books. After each girl finished her book, she then exchanged them with the others so everyone could be sure to read all the available titles.

The popular series came to life in 1930; as some historians have noted, the books debuted not more than a decade after women got the right to vote. Some view the teenage sleuth as "America's first feminist." The books, written by numerous authors under the pen name Carolyn Keene, were aimed at girls between the ages of 8 and 12; their success was astonishing and the series became hugely popular throughout the 1930s, 1940s, and 1950s.[21]

The premise of the books was simple: teenager Nancy Drew lived in the Midwestern town of River Heights with her father, Carson Drew, a highly successful lawyer and a widower, and the Drew's housekeeper Hannah Gruen. Aided by her friend Bess and Bess's tomboy cousin George, Nancy embarks on a series of adventures following clues and solving mysteries that involved anything from stolen jewels to a missing prince. She has a boyfriend, who tries his best to boss her, but clearly it is Nancy who is in charge.[22]

Nancy Drew's appeal was clear to young readers: she was smart, brave, resourceful, and independent. Nancy was also determined and persistent; no matter the obstacle or problem, she always persevered and succeeded. For Sonia Sotomayor, Nancy Drew represented boldness and intelligence, and she decided early that when she grew up, she wanted to be a detective, just like her literary heroine.[23]

Unfortunately, with her diabetes, that dream would not be possible; Sotomayor was told that being a detective was too arduous a career for someone in her condition. But Sotomayor was not easily dissuaded. She had surmised that somehow she had a destiny to fulfill; if she was not entirely clear about what form it was to take, it was certainly not for lack of trying to figure out her life plan.

If she could not be a detective, Sotomayor reasoned, there were other options that proved just as appealing. In addition to her interest in solving mysteries and thwarting crime, which the Nancy Drew books had cultivated, Sotomayor loved the popular television program *Perry Mason*, which was broadcast on Thursday nights. Mason was a defense attorney who week after week matched wits and legal strategy against the local District Attorney Hamilton Burger by defending clients who had been wrongly accused of a crime. She remembered one of Mason's courtroom rivals telling him, "Justice is served when a guilty man is convicted and when an innocent man is not." "That TV character said something that molded my life," Sotomayor said later.[24]

For Sotomayor, it was as if a door had been kicked open. She may not have been strong enough to be a detective, but lawyers did not need physical prowess to win justice and solve crimes. Her direction seemed clear: she would pursue a career in law. But she decided that she wanted to do more than argue cases in court in the name of justice. In fact, there was one other person in the courtroom who had even greater power and influence. As she recalled many years later, "I thought, what a wonderful occupation to have. And I made the quantum leap: If that was the prosecutor's job, then the guy who made the decision to dismiss the case was the judge. That was what I was going to be."[25]

Sotomayor's retreat into reading and television offset some of the more somber aspects of her life. Both she and her brother still needed looking after, which was provided either by her mother's friend Ana or her father's mother, grandmother Mercedes. When they were not available, Celina would drop the children off with one of her late husband's sisters, who worked in a sweatshop. It was a harrowing existence that left a strong impression on Sotomayor.

As she entered the shop, Sotomayor noticed how dark and hot the room was; even the windows were blacked out. Sotomayor recalled in a 2007 speech that "I struggled all day to get to the door to smell some fresh air and see light. . . . Titi would vigilantly chase me away from the door all day long. Little did I know then that the shop and its employees were hiding themselves from the police." The horrible conditions and paltry wages were normal for many Puerto Rican women in New York City, who struggled to make a living doing piecework for sewing and needlework companies.[26]

Offsetting this memory though, were the trips to Puerto Rico where Celina and the children would visit Celina's family in the towns of Mayagues and Lajas. During this period, flights to Puerto Rico were quite cheap and Celina made the most of these trips. There were drives to Cabo Rojo, located on the west coast of the island where the family took boat rides to the Isla de Ratones, or Mouse Island. Here the Sotomayor children and their cousins played in the sand and frolicked in the waters.

SCHOOL DAYS

One thing constant in Sotomayor's childhood was her mother's emphasis on learning. "I don't care what you do," she would tell her children, "but be the best at it." To be the best student, one had to study hard; both the Sotomayor children took their mother's advice to heart and applied themselves to their schoolwork. Monday through Friday, the two children attended Blessed Sacrament School, a Catholic school located on Beach Avenue, about two miles from the Bronxdale Houses community. Both Sotomayor and her brother attended the beige brick building from kindergarten to eighth grade.

During her school years, Sotomayor was noted as an increasingly confident young girl, and as a student who was willing and able, to express ideas and opinions on a variety of subjects. More than one friend recalled that when Sotomayor spoke of things she was interested in, she felt them deeply and was passionate about her beliefs. Sotomayor earned a reputation as an excellent student with perfect attendance, and she graduated at the top of the eighth-grade class of 1968.[27]

In addition to their studies, the students at Blessed Sacrament benefited from the tutelage of two priests: Father Marty Dolan and Father Vinny Gorman. Both men were committed to helping their young charges to learn and respect the different cultural backgrounds of the students at the school and in the world beyond. Father Dolan often took students on weekend outings to expose them to the opportunities and challenges of the world. Paul La Rosa, a former student at Blessed Sacrament, described the outings as an opportunity to see the world outside of the Bronx. More important, the children were exposed to other children of different racial and ethnic backgrounds including children of Irish, Italian, Latino, and African American descents. These outings also offered the priests another opportunity to teach the students the importance of getting along with others from different backgrounds.[28]

Celina's drive to make sure that her children had the best opportunities she could provide led to one of the most important purchases in the Sotomayor household: a set of *Encyclopedia Britannica*. Celina "was famous for the encyclopedia," said Milagros Baez O'Toole, a cousin. The multivolume set was expensive; the Sotomayors were the only family in the projects to own a set. Sotomayor recounted in a 1999 commencement speech the sacrifices her mother made for her children's education:

> For my mother, education has always been the top priority in all our lives. . . . When I was growing up, the Encyclopedia was a home library—a series of books filled with articles and beautiful pictures about almost anything you wanted to know about. Most of you can't imagine what it was like—the days before color tv— to open up those wonderful books and stare at those beautifully colored and educational pictures. Despite the enormous financial burden that purchase placed on my mother, we had those wonderful books.[29]

The books were treated with great respect in the Sotomayor household. Both children knew how their mother struggled to make the payments. At the same time, Sonia later joked that the encyclopedia provided them the opportunity to plagiarize many of their school reports. Still, both children were aware of the sacrifices made on their behalf by their mother who wanted nothing more than to give them opportunities that she did not have as a child.[30]

It was clear that much was expected of Sotomayor: not only from her mother, but also from her other female relatives. As her brother stated, "The females were expected to achieve more." That meant his sister needed to be applying herself all the time. There could be little respite. At one point, when her aunts and grandmother discovered that

Sotomayor was spending her time reading comic books, they conferred with Celina, expressing their concerns that such reading would distract Sotomayor from her studies.[31]

CHANGING TIMES

Unfortunately, by the mid-1960s, the Southview neighborhood was undergoing dramatic changes—none for the good. Where the Bronxdale Houses had once been the scene of family get-togethers and play outings for children, there were now drugs and street gangs. For Juan particularly, the neighborhood had become a source of trouble; his bicycle was stolen and he was mugged on a number of occasions. His older sister did her best to protect him. As he remembered later, his sister "was tough as nails": "My sister always had to come over and defuse situations. Like a natural diplomat, she tried negotiation first and, if words didn't work would move on to step two."[32] Juan recalled one episode where he was surrounded by kids and his sister came to his rescue, saying, "Listen if you're going to beat him up you got to beat me up too."[33]

Describing the old neighborhood, Sotomayor was thoughtful in her appraisal of what was happening; for many, it boiled down to choices. "There were working poor in the projects," she said in a 1998 interview. "There were poor poor in the projects. There were sick poor in the projects. There were addicts and non-addicts and all sorts of people, every one of them with problems, and each group with a different response, different methods of survival, different reactions to the adversity they were facing. And you saw kids making choices."[34]

During this period, Sotomayor took on her first part-time job working at Zaro's Bakery, which was located about 10 blocks from where she lived. She proved to be an industrious and tireless worker, so much so, that her brother later complained that she proved a difficult act to follow when he began working there. From Zaro's, Sotomayor began working at United Bargains during the summer to earn extra money. In the meantime, Celina began looking for another place to live as the neighborhood was becoming more dangerous. She was committed to getting her children out of the neighborhood so that they would not be tempted to go astray or be harmed if they resisted temptation.[35]

HIGH SCHOOL

In 1968, Sotomayor took the required high school entrance exam and found out she had been accepted to Cardinal Spellman High School, one of the top Catholic schools in the city. The school was located approximately five miles from the Bronxdale Houses. Although the majority of the student body was white, there were a small number of African American and Hispanic students. The student body was divided into Boys and Girls Departments; each section had its own principal, teachers, and classrooms. The boys were taught by priests and male faculty, the girls by nuns and women. However, boys and girls could eat together in the school cafeteria and participate in co-ed school activities. The school's motto was simple but direct: *Sequere Deum*, Follow God.[36]

The school had a top-notch curriculum, and for Sotomayor the discipline and classes were both challenging and rewarding. Other classmates remember Sotomayor as extremely focused. She soon developed a reputation as one of the top students in the school. One recalled that "She was irrepressible, very popular, very bright, very dynamic. . . . She wasn't overbearing about it, but you knew she was in the room."[37] She participated in school government and was a member of the debate team. Many credit her stable home life as contributing mightily to her success; instead of spending time on the streets, Sotomayor was dedicated to her studies as well as helping out at home and working part-time to earn extra money.[38]

Many years later, Ted Shaw, in giving testimony before the Senate Judiciary Committee on behalf of Sotomayor's nomination to the Supreme Court described his former classmate:

> Sonia was at the top of our class at Cardinal Spellman High School. Everyone—white, black, Latino, Asian—ranked behind her. She was studious, independent-minded, mature beyond her years, thoughtful, and was not easily influenced by what was going on around her. Sonia walked her own path. . . . Sonia was a leader at Cardinal Spellman. She was active in school governance and on the debate team. But more than anything, Sonia led by her excellence. Sonia Sotomayor set the pace at which others wanted to run.[39]

CO-OP CITY AND A NEW DIRECTION

In the winter of 1970, when Sotomayor was a sophomore, Celina moved her family out of Bronxdale Houses. The neighborhood had continued to decline with drug dealers and street gangs; crime was on the rise. Landlords set fire to their building to collect insurance money. The once pristine housing developments—the promise of urban renewal and a better life for so many working people—had deteriorated into crime-infested, graffiti-ridden buildings surrounded by rubble and decay.

Celine found a home in the new housing development known as Co-op City, located in the northeast section of the Bronx between the New England Thruway and the Hutchinson River. The development had opened in 1968 and was the largest apartment development of its kind in the country. It included 35 towers, some at a height of 33 stories. The project included 15,372 units, situated along 338 acres of marshland and seven townhouse clusters, each with 33 units.[40]

Co-op City, often described as a "city within a city," was built under New York State's 1955 Limited Profit Housing Law, which financed moderate-income housing. Before developers broke ground for Co-op City in 1966, the land was the site of a short-lived, financially troubled theme park, Freedomland USA. From the very beginning, Co-op City was a racially diverse community that attracted residents of different religions and nationalities all seeking one thing: home ownership. In addition to the housing units, Co-op City also boasted four schools, a post office, a fire station, a library, and playgrounds. There were three shopping centers, each with its own supermarket, a dry cleaner, restaurants, shops, and community rooms for cultural events and private parties. A 25-acre educational park counted among its offerings a planetarium. There were also different churches and other religious facilities for residents.[41]

Celina bought a two-bedroom apartment for $2,025 down and payments of $116 a month. According to a promotional brochure, Co-op City's units promised "maximum light and privacy" with "light cheerful kitchens with large refrigerators, ranges, [and] wood-grained plastic-finish cabinets." The unit was also close to Cardinal Spellman High School, which meant that Sotomayor and her brother had only to take a 15 minute bus ride that ended a block from the school. Like the

Bronxdale Houses, moving to Co-op City was another step up for the Sotomayors.[42]

The family quickly settled into their new home, where Celina soon made many friends. Even though she was still working six days a week, she always had time to help out friends and even became an unofficial caretaker and nurse for those residents who needed help, company, or just to see a friendly face. Sotomayor's home was also open to friends. At any given time, students from immigrant families mingled with wealthier students from Westchester County. The teens engaged in all manner of debates: school gossip, the war in Vietnam, current events, race relations, and social justice. Ken Moy, a classmate of Sotomayor's at Cardinal Spellman, remembers many good times at the Sotomayor house, where he was a regular visitor, spending many evenings in the kitchen with Sonia and her family.[43]

What Moy remembers most about those times was Celina bustling about fixing meals for her children's friends. "I can't tell you how many times I said, 'Is there another pork chop?'" he said many years later, "and there was." Moy also remembers his friend "presiding" at the kitchen table, offering advice on a wide range of subjects to friends and family. Even then, Moy remembered, she had the makings and bearing of a judge: "She was very analytical, even back then. It was clear to people who knew her that if she wasn't going to be a lawyer, she was going to be in public life somehow."[44]

NEW DIRECTIONS FOR CELINA

By Sotomayor's junior year in high school, Celina had some decisions to make. Even though she was earning a good salary at the hospital, she also knew that there would come a time when she would need to earn more money. As Sotomayor remembered: "In my junior year of high school, my mother sat our family down to talk about the future. She knew that we would leave home in only a few years and that my father's Social Security benefits would end shortly. She asked us whether we could make the sacrifice of her going to college so that she could become a registered nurse."[45]

As far as Sotomayor and her brother were concerned, her mother's wish to return to school was not an issue. Sotomayor remembers how dedicated her mother was with her studies; as soon as she returned home from work or her classes, she began her studying, often staying up until the late hours. Celina earned straight A's in her studies and as Sotomayor said years later, watching her mother meant that she and her brother had to study extra hard. Many evenings found all three reading and writing around the kitchen table. When the time came to take the nursing test, Celina passed the difficult five-part exam on her first try, as she had done with her GED years earlier.[46]

SENIOR YEAR

By the time Sotomayor was a senior, she was starting to think about the possibility of attending college. Unlike some of her classmates who were thinking of attending a state school, Sotomayor decided to shoot for the moon and apply to several Ivy League universities even though she admitted that "I didn't know what an Ivy League college was." But then she saw the popular movie *Love Story* about a romance between Harvard students. Sotomayor was entranced by the Harvard campus. "I saw the university on the screen and I thought to myself, what a magical-looking place," she recalled.

She traveled to Boston to interview for admission to Harvard. When she arrived, she was overwhelmed by her meeting with an admissions officer who invited her into an office featuring a white sofa, an expensive looking oriental carpet, and two yapping toy poodles. "I fled," she later said. She then visited Yale in New Haven, Connecticut, where she was invited to join an antiwar protest. This experience was very unsettling for Sotomayor who is a self-proclaimed rule-follower. Instead, Sotomayor decided to try for Princeton, where her friend Ken Moy had been accepted the previous year.[47]

The son of Chinese immigrants, Moy was blunt with Sotomayor. He told her that if accepted, she would be an outsider at Princeton. He remembers telling her, "I don't want you to come here with any illusions. Social isolation is going to be a part of your experience, and you have to have the strength of character to get through intact." Moy also encouraged Sotomayor to apply for financial aid. To everyone's delight, Sotomayor was accepted for admission to every college she applied for, including Princeton, for the fall of 1972. It was a tremendous victory and accomplishment for the entire family and a true testament to the powerful influence that Celina exerted over her children.[48]

Her last duty at Cardinal Spellman was to give the valedictorian address to the graduating class. After that, Sotomayor was bound for a new world where new opportunities and new challenges awaited her. It would also mean a deep and intense journey of discovery—not only about her future, but also her very identity.

NOTES

1. "Puerto Rican Emigration: Why the 1950s?," http://lcw.lehman.edu/lehman/depts/latinampuertorican/latinoweb/PuertoRico/1950s.htm.

2. Ibid.

3. Ibid.

4. "Puerto Rican Labor Movement," http://chnm.gmu.edu/wwh/modules/lesson16/lesson16.php?s=0.

5. Ibid.

6. "Soundview, Bronx," http://en.wikipedia.org/wiki/Soundview,_Bronx.

7. "Bronxdale Houses," http://www.nyc.gov/html/nycha/html/developments/bronxdalehouses.shtml; Robin Shulman, "Sonia Sotomayor Built Successful Life on Then-Solid Ground of Bronxdale Houses," *Washington Post,* June 16, 2009, http://www.washingtonpost.com/wp-dyn/content/article/2009/06/15/AR2009061503170.html.

8. Sheryl Gay Stolberg, "Sotomayor, a Trailblazer and Dreamer," *New York Times*, May 26, 2009, http://www.nytimes.com/2009/05/27/us/politics/27websotomayor.html?pagewanted=all.

9. Antonia Felix, *Sonia Sotomayor: The True American Dream*, New York: Berkeley Publishing Group, 2010, p 16; Shulman, "Sonia Sotomayor Built Successful Life on Then-Solid Ground of Bronxdale Houses."

10. "A Biographical Sketch of Sonia Sotomayor," *YouTube*, http://www.youtube.com/watch?v=yYjuS-d8PL8.

11. Ibid.

12. Shulman, "Sonia Sotomayor Built Successful Life on Then-Solid Ground of Bronxdale Houses."

13. Ibid.; Felix, *Sonia Sotomayor*, pp. 18–19.

14. Sonia Sotomayor, "A Latina Judges Voice," *New York Times*, May 14, 2009, http://www.nytimes.com/2009/05/15/us/politics/15judge. text.html?pagewanted=all.

15. Shulman, "Sonia Sotomayor Built Successful Life on Then-Solid Ground of Bronxdale Houses."

16. Christine Mai-Duc, "Sonia Sotomayor Discusses Her Diabetes with Children's Group," *Los Angeles Times*, June 21, 2011, http://www. latimes.com/health/la-na-sotomayor-diabetes-20110622,0,6515717. story.

17. Joan Biskupic, "Sotomayor Opens Up about Her Diabetes," *USA Today*, June 24, 2011, http://www.usatoday.com/news/washing ton/judicial/supremecourtjustices/2011–06–21-sotomayor-diabetes-court_n.htm; Mai-Duc, "Sonia Sotomayor Discusses her Diabetes with Children's Group."

18. Ibid.

19. Ibid.

20. Felix, *Sonia Sotomayor*, p. 20.

21. Jan Hoffman, "Nancy Drew's Granddaughters," *New York Times*, July 17, 2009, http://www.nytimes.com/2009/07/19/fashion/19drew. html?pagewanted=all.

22. Ibid.

23. Ibid.

24. Joan Biskupic and Kathy Kiely, "Perry Masons' Stories 'Molded' Sotomayor," *USA Today*, July 23, 2009, http://www.usatoday.com/ news/washington/judicial/2009–07–15-sotomayor-video-hearing_N. htm.

25. Jan Hoffman, "A Breakthrough Judge; What She Always Wanted," *New York Times*, September 25, 1992, http://www.nytimes. com/1992/09/25/news/a-breakthrough-judge-what-she-always-wanted. html.

26. Laurie Kelliman, "Sotomayor Speeches Detail Life, Uncertain-ties," *Salt Lake Tribune*, June 5, 2009, http://archive.sltrib.com/article. php?id=12527117&itype=NGPSID&keyword=&qtype=.

27. Manny Fernandez, "The Children at the Judge's Bronx School," *New York Times*, July 15, 2009, http://www.nytimes.com/2009/07/16/ nyregion/16bronx.html?ref=nyregion.

28. Felix, *Sonia Sotomayor*, p. 26.

29. Sonia Sotomayor, "Remarks Prepared for Delivery at the Lehman College Commencement," June 3, 1999, http://www.lehman.cuny.edu/lehman/enews/2009_05_18/pdf/sotomayor_remarks.pdf.

30. Felix, *Sonia Sotomayor*, p. 25.

31. Ibid., p. 24.

32. Jason Carroll, "Growing Up Sotomayor" July 13, 2009, http://am.blogs.cnn.com/2009/07/13/growing-up-sotomayor/.

33. Sandra Sobieraj Westfall, "Sonia Sotomayor: From the Bronx to the Bench," *People*, August 17, 2009, p. 75.

34. Stolberg, "Sotomayor, a Trailblazer and Dreamer."

35. Felix, *Sonia Sotomayor*, p. 26.

36. Ibid., pp. 26–27.

37. Stolberg, "Sotomayor, a Trailblazer and Dreamer."

38. Felix, *Sonia Sotomayor*, p. 28.

39. "Testimony of Theodore Shaw," July 16, 2009, http://judiciary.senate.gov/hearings/testimony.cfm?id=e655f9e2809e5476862f735da14d3b3b&wit_id=e655f9e2809e5476862f735da14d3b3b-4-3.

40. Elsa Brenner, "Everything You Need in one Giant Package," *New York Times*, April 6, 2008, http://www.nytimes.com/2008/04/06/realestate/06live.html.

41. Ibid.

42. Ibid.; Felix, *Sonia Sotomayor*, p. 29.

43. Stolberg, "Sotomayor, a Trailblazer and Dreamer."

44. "Induction Proceedings for Judge Sonia Sotomayor, November 6, 1998," United States Court House, 500 Pearl Street, New York, NY; Stolberg, "Sotomayor, a Trailblazer and Dreamer.".

45. "Induction Proceedings for Judge Sonia Sotomayor, November 6, 1998."

46. Ibid.

47. Kathy Kiely, "No Dissent: A Locomotive for Sotomayor '76," June 1, 2011, http://paw.princeton.edu/issues/2011/06/01/pages/4772/index.xml.

48. Stolberg, "Sotomayor, a Trailblazer and Dreamer."

Chapter 3

PRINCETON DAYS

Sonia Sotomayor spent her first week at Princeton University obsessing over the sound of a cricket. As a child of the housing projects in the Bronx, the rhythmic chirpings of the tiny insect was just one of many new experiences awaiting there. Friends recall how she tore her dorm room apart looking for whatever was causing the noise. Sotomayor, recalling that event in 2002, then explained how her only connection to a cricket came from watching the popular Disney character, Jiminy Cricket from the movie *Pinocchio*. It would take her boyfriend and future husband, Kevin Noonan, to finally explain to the frustrated Sotomayor that the cricket was not in her room but outside. As Sotomayor declared later, "This was all new to me: we didn't have trees brushing up against windows in the South Bronx."[1]

"IN THE NATION'S SERVICE"

Chartered in 1746 as the College of New Jersey, Princeton University was the fourth college established in British North America. It had been chartered in the name of King George II "for the Education of Youth in the Learned Languages and in the Liberal Arts and Sciences."

Its doors were to be open to all students, "any different sentiments in religion notwithstanding." The purpose of the college was to train men who would become "ornaments of the State as well as the Church."[2]

The institution was originally located in Elizabeth, New Jersey, where its first president, the Reverend Jonathan Dickinson, also served as pastor of the town's Presbyterian church. Unfortunately, Dickinson died within a few months after the school opened its doors. In May 1747, Reverend Aaron Burr, then-pastor of the Presbyterian church in Newark, was persuaded to take on the duties as president of the college. Burr then decided to move the college to Newark that fall; by spring of 1748, the college had its first graduating class of six young men.[3]

In the fall of 1756, Burr moved the college to Princeton. The students and their teachers were housed in Nassau Hall, then one of the largest stone buildings built in America. The land for the school was donated by Nathaniel FitzRandolph; the building's name was from the House of Nassau, the family of the then English King and prince of Orange, William III. The building would have other functions besides that of an educational institution; during the Revolutionary War, Nassau Hall served as a military hospital or barracks that housed both British and American troops.[4]

At war's end, Nassau Hall was also the scene of important political gatherings including the first session of the New Jersey state legislature and the Continental Congress. The college received its current name in 1896, when the school's continued expansion of its courses elevated the school to university status. The College of New Jersey was officially renamed Princeton University in honor of its host community of Princeton.[5]

NEW WORLDS

The world Sonia Sotomayor entered in the fall of 1972 was unlike anything she had encountered so far. The beautifully landscaped grounds of the college with its Gothic architecture and overwhelmingly white student body made Sotomayor feel out of place and increased her sense of loneliness. During her first week on campus, she holed up in her room. It did not help matters either that Sotomayor was made to feel different. On her very first day, a Southern girl turned to her and two other Hispanic girls and said how wonderful it was that Princeton had all these strange people.[6]

"She did mention that, as a freshman, she felt sometimes intimidated by others and didn't really raise her hand very much," stated a classmate. As a first-year student, Sotomayor felt what she's called a "chasm" between herself and her classmates, and was unsure of herself in this new world. Many of the students came from privileged backgrounds, and would often talk about their vacations in Europe or holidays spent skiing, experiences that were far removed from Sotomayor's experiences growing up in the Bronx. Sotomayor stood out for another reason; she was one of a handful of women attending the college. Her arrival at Princeton marked the third year the university admitted women. She was also among a very small minority of Latino students; the class of 1976 that totaled 1,127 counted among its minorities, 22 Latino students, 15 Chicano students, and 113 African American students.[7]

Sotomayor was also plagued by her own self-doubts as to whether she belonged at Princeton. During a panel discussion in 1990, Sotomayor stated that she felt she was a "product of affirmative action" and questioned whether she would have been accepted into Princeton based on her test scores alone. She explained to the audience that "I am a product of affirmative action. . . . I am the perfect affirmative action baby. I am Puerto Rican, born and raised in the south Bronx. My test scores were not comparable to my colleagues at Princeton and Yale. Not so far off so that I wasn't able to succeed at those institutions."[8]

However, according to Sotomayor's biographer, Antonia Felix, Sotomayor, even if a beneficiary of affirmative action, still would have had to make a very favorable impression to be admitted to the college. At the time that Sotomayor applied, the Princeton admissions guidelines were structured in such a way that there was a fixed ratio of four men accepted for every woman. What this translated into was that only 14 percent of female applicants were admitted to Princeton compared to 22 percent of its male applicants. Sotomayor may have benefited from affirmative action, but only up to a point. Clearly, she was among the more elite applicants that were accepted by the college.[9]

SETTLING IN

As a freshman, Sotomayor roomed with Dolores Chavez, a Mexican American from Albuquerque, New Mexico. The pair lived in Walker Hall. As Chavez recalled, "It was like a small-town girl meets this big-city-woman type of thing." Chavez was an exuberant personality; she made curtains on her sewing machine for their dorm room and introduced Sotomayor to tacos and played the folk song "La Paloma" on the guitar. Chavez also remembered that the "First thing [Sotomayor] said was 'Dolores, you're from New Mexico. You smile way too much.'"[10]

In addition to her studies, Sotomayor worked in the school cafeteria on the steam line. A former student, Nick Allard, who worked with Sotomayor remembers that the student employees were required to wear a blue button-down shirt with a "dorky bow tie and a name tag.... "The more juvenile of us would wear the bow tie halfway off, or have the shirttail out," Allard stated. But Sotomayor, ever the stickler for rules, was different. According to Allard, "Sonia would show up, wearing it [the uniform] properly. It was clear that she had bigger fish to fry."[11]

Though she felt like "an alien in a very strange land" when she arrived in Princeton, Sotomayor said Princeton "became a home that was so foundational for my growth later on." Even though she was, in many classes, the only woman in the room, she soon began earning a reputation as a thoughtful student and a hard worker. Another student described Sotomayor as: "at first seemingly meek, quiet, and brainy. All of us knew early on that she was driven. Part of the drive stemmed from a need to prove that she was equal to those from privileged backgrounds. Sonia could not only 'keep up,' she beat them at their own game by excelling beyond students of all backgrounds."[12]

In spite of her hard work, Sotomayor realized that although she had been an excellent student at both of her schools in the Bronx, Princeton had another, higher set of standards.

A PIVOTAL MEETING

Peter Winn, a history professor at Princeton remembered the first time he met Sonia Sotomayor:

The first time she walked into my office in Princeton University's Dickinson Hall, Sonia Sotomayor was holding a paper she'd written for my Contemporary Latin America course. It was marked up with my corrections in red ink. Spanish was her first language, and many of her errors reflected its syntax. Where she had written "dictatorship of authority," I had scribbled "authoritarian dictatorship." That sort of mistake is common when students use different languages at home and at school. Less common was Sonia's determination to overcome this challenge.[13]

That initial encounter marked the beginning of a strong mentoring relationship for Sotomayor during her time at Princeton.

Over the course of the next three years, Sotomayor worked closely with Winn on her studies. As a history major, Sotomayor's classes were quite intensive and there was a great deal of writing to be done. She knew if she was to succeed, it was vital to close the gap that existed between her writing skills and that of other students. Winn admitted that Sotomayor was not the best student he had ever taught, but what struck him the most was that she was a student who did not believe in wasting opportunities when they were offered. She was a frequent visitor to Winn's office where the two would meticulously go through her papers so that Sotomayor could see where improvement was needed. Winn went over the finer points of grammar and the two also talked about history. The two also discussed the fact that there were no classes on Latino history.[14]

Over the course of her college career, Sotomayor took five courses with Winn, including the writing of her senior thesis. According to Winn, Sotomayor underwent a dramatic transformation from "a tentative teenager—so intimidated that she never spoke in class during her first semester" to that of a "poised young woman who negotiated successfully with top university administrators on contentious issues such as minority hiring practices."[15]

ACCIÓN PUERTORRIQUEÑA

Even as she threw herself into her studies, Sotomayor found the time to become involved in some campus activities. These included the

Third World Center and the Committee on Discipline. Sotomayor, along with other students, also volunteered at the Trenton Psychiatric Hospital to provide Spanish speaking skills. She would also help to organize a Latino students' organization. All of her choices were carefully thought out; one student described her as a person who "was slow to join things. She sized things up for a while before she decided to become a part of something . . . I had a sense she was very methodical in her decision-making."[16]

Sotomayor's activities, particularly those with the Acción Puertorriqueña (Puerto Rican Action), coincided with a wave of Latino student political activism that was sweeping across many college campuses during the 1960s and 1970s. In general, many college students during this period believed it was time for a revolution; according to a poll taken by the New York Times during the summer of 1970, nearly 40 percent of American college students (or approximately three million people) believed that a revolution was necessary if certain social, economic, and political changes were to succeed. At the forefront of those calling for change were a number of Latino student organizations that were active on college campuses from coast to coast.[17]

Unlike African Americans who had their own historically black colleges and universities that had a deep activist tradition, Latino and Latina students had nothing. Because of this it took quite some time for a critical mass of students to arrive on college campuses that would allow the creation of student activist movement. That is not to say that Latino and Latina young adults did nothing; many gave their energies to activist groups seeking change in neighborhoods and workplaces.[18]

Finally, by the late 1960s and 1970s, Puerto Rican and Mexican American students began demanding changes on college campuses. These included the end of discriminatory practices, a more inclusive curriculum and better access to educational institutions. Using walkouts, sit-ins, demonstrations, conferences, and other forms of peaceful resistance, these student groups lobbied hard for changes on college campuses, particularly on the east and west coasts.

At Princeton, Latino students had a difficult time, even more so than African American students. At that time, the university appeared to be more committed to conquering problems with black students than those with other minorities. This was aided in part by the fact that the town had an African American population, but no real Latino community. And while Latino students had attended the university before Sotomayor's class, it was her class that sought out its cultural identity. As one of Sotomayor's professors wrote many years later: "They were few in number, young and homesick, without the sounds or tastes of home. All students complain about cafeteria food, but the Latino students' complaints were about identity, not quality—about how alien Princeton felt to them. Sonia told me she had never been so aware of being different."[19]

Sotomayor, who initially had to be coaxed to join Acción Puertorriqueña, would by her sophomore year become co-chair of the organization. Among her activities with the group was to lead a campaign to get Princeton to hire more Latino faculty members and admit more Latino students. Among the student complaints were that the university had no administrators or faculty members of either a Puerto Rican or Chicano background. Not only that but there were few Latino students and the university offered no courses dealing with Latino and Chicano histories or cultures.

At first, the Latino students had little success with their campaign. Then in 1974, Acción Puertorriqueña working with the Chicano Organization of Princeton, filed a formal complaint with the Department of Health, Education, and Welfare. According to the student newspaper, the *Daily Princetonian*, the groups charged the university "with a 'lack of commitment' in hiring Puerto Rican and Chicano administrators and faculty and recruiting students from these minority groups."[20]

Sotomayor threw herself into the frontlines of the battle. In her May 10, 1974, letter to the editor of the *Daily Princetonian*, she charged the university with an "institutional pattern of discrimination."[21] The work of the coalition paid off in that their efforts were in part responsible for hiring a Latino as assistant dean of student affairs later that year, with Sotomayor and some other minority students serving on a student advisory committee for the job search. Sotomayor learned other valuable skills as well such as the value of building coalitions, persuading students to defend their values and realizing that the law could be used an instrument of social change.

During those days, many students in the organization found Sotomayor to be the "voice of reason. . . . There were Hispanics who felt
that we shouldn't be in dialogue with the administration—we ought to
be telling them to take a hike." But Sotomayor's suggestions to take the
legal way as a means of solving the problem in the end proved to be an
effective tactic. Not only did it get the administration's attention, but
the administrators also began paying closer attention as to how they
recruited minorities.[22]

IN SEARCH OF AN IDENTITY

It was also at Princeton that Sonia Sotomayor fully explored her own
ethnic identity as a Latina woman and a Nyurican (a New York City
Puerto Rican). In addition to her social activism, Sotomayor took
classes about the history of Puerto Rico. One result of the Acción
Puertorriqueña advocating more classes on Latino culture and history
was the addition in the spring of 1974, of a seminar on the history
and politics of Puerto Rico and mainland Puerto Ricans. Her mentor
Professor Winn was asked to teach the class. Winn was skeptical about
undertaking the class; he had no background in the subject and was
not of Latino or Puerto Rican heritage. But Sotomayor believed that
he was the best person for the job and she was finally able to convince
Winn to teach the class.

For the Latino students, the seminar was the first step in what they
hoped would be the creation of a Latino Studies curriculum at Princeton, taught by Latino faculty. The class was small, consisting of 15 students, most of who were of Puerto Rican heritage, but there were a few
other Latinos and white Americans. One highlight of the class was
a collaborative research project on the Puerto Rican community in
nearby Trenton. Among the tasks the students undertook was a map-
ping of the community, analyzing its demographics as well as undertaking oral histories of community members. It was hoped that the class
would serve as a model for other community histories. According to
Winn though, one of the highlights of the class was finding a Puerto
Rican restaurant in Trenton.[23]

For their final papers, the students were asked to do oral histories of
their own families, which included the migration experiences of com-

ing to America. For Sotomayor, the class was a revelation. Not only did she learn about how to conduct oral histories, but she also continued to improve on her research and writing skills. But the assignment also had a personal benefit for her; in the course of her studies, she interviewed many relatives, who later passed on. The assignment gave Sotomayor and her brother the only real history of their extended family.[24]

Winn believes that the seminar also helped Sotomayor grapple with her own identity as a Nuyorican from the Bronx rather than a "Puerto Rican from the island." He also remembers Sotomayor's transformation from a shy and somewhat awkward freshman to that of a confident and articulate young woman. Engaged by the class material and her classmates, Sotomayor was often found having passionate discussions about issues surrounding Puerto Rico such as statehood, the identity of the island as an autonomous commonwealth, and potential independence. The class provided a rich field of discussion and research that would play a vital role in Sotomayor's senior thesis.

SENIOR YEAR

Sotomayor was also making a name for herself in other classes such as Jameson Doig's public policy class, "The Politics of Economic and Social Control." The class, which met three times a week, always began in the same fashion, with Doig offering a 15 to 20 minute presentation on some topic that concerned public policy, such as housing, prisons, education, and environmental regulations. After the conclusion of his findings, Doig's students were encouraged to share their views. Some topics such as police brutality had a special resonance for students like Sotomayor who had grown up in areas where crime was a constant problem. Doig remembers her as being extremely articulate in describing her concerns over many of the problems and policy discussed in class. It was no coincidence either that Doig's class was a popular one for students, including Sotomayor, who were considering law school.[25]

By her senior year, Sotomayor had emerged as a straight-A student in her classes. She was also ready to undertake another challenging project: her senior thesis. Working again under Professor Winn, Sotomayor chose Luis Muñoz Marín, a Puerto Rican poet, journalist, and politician, who is regarded as the "father of modern Puerto Rico" as her topic. Marín was the first democratically elected governor of Puerto Rico, who among other things helped to create the Constitution for Puerto Rico, which moved the status of the country to a commonwealth. Marín was an able politician and a popular governor, and served a total of 16 years as governor, all of them representing the Popular Democratic Party.

According to Winn, Sotomayor's topic was an ambitious one and her paper was longer than the average senior thesis. It also turned out to be the best paper she had ever written for Winn. He wrote that Sotomayor's argument "carefully reasoned and supported by evidence from diverse sources—is the kind of judicious analysis that might have led a clairvoyant reader to predict a successful career on the bench." Sotomayor was also happy to note that the second reader for her thesis—a professor that she had not worked with very much—told her it was the best-written senior thesis he had ever read.[26]

Sotomayor's senior thesis capped what had been an exceptional academic career. In her last two years at Princeton, she not only made straight A's in all her subjects, but in her comprehensive history exams, she also received an A-plus from the most difficult grader in the history department. She graduated Phi Beta Kappa and *summa cum laude*, the highest honors that a senior undergraduate can receive. As a final honor Sotomayor received the Pyne Prize, the highest award given to a graduating senior. Sotomayor was also the first Latina to receive the award.

Sotomayor's triumph at Princeton was a personal and political triumph for her. She overcame serious obstacles during the course of her academic career and emerged as a polished, well-respected, and articulate student leader. She had learned hard lessons of diplomacy, compromise, and to push forward to overcome barriers of many different kinds. Now, with diploma in hand, she was headed to another Ivy League Ivory tower: Yale Law School. She would never completely shed her sense of not fitting in; but instead of using it to cover up any deficiencies she might have felt she had, she used it as a way to distinguish herself, to make herself heard and to always keep moving forward.

NOTES

1. Elizabeth Landau, "Cricket, Ivy League Classmates Startled Student Sonia Sotomayor," *CNN*, July 15, 2009, http://articles.cnn.

com/2009–07–15/us/sotomayor.college_1_cricket-sonia-sotomayor-classmates?_s=PM:US.

2. Princeton University, "Princeton University at a Glance," http://www.princeton.edu/main/about/history/glance/.

3. Ibid.

4. Ibid.

5. Ibid.

6. Evan Thomas, Stuart Taylor Jr., and Brian No, "Meet the Sotomayors," *Newsweek*, July 20, 2009, p. 43.

7. Landau, "Cricket, Ivy League Classmates Startled Student Sonia Sotomayor."

8. Bill Mears, "Sotomayor Says She was the 'Perfect Affirmative Action Baby,'" *CNNPolitics*, June 11, 2009, http://articles.cnn.com/2009–06–11/politics/sotomayor.affirmative.action_1_affirmative-action-wise-latina-woman-test-scores?_s=PM:POLITICS.

9. Antonia Felix, *Sonia Sotomayor: The True American Dream*, New York: Berkeley Publishing Group, 2010, p. 38.

10. Lauren Collins, "Number Nine: Sonia Sotomayor's High Profile Debut," *New Yorker*, January 11, 2010, p. 42.

11. Ibid.

12. Brett Tomlinson, "Sotomayor in PAW," *Princeton Alumni Weekly*, July 13, 2009, http://blogs.princeton.edu/paw/2009/07/sotomayor_in_pa.html.

13. Peter Winn, "Mentor at Princeton Recalls Sotomayor's Evolution," *The Washington Post*, July 12, 2009, http://www.washingtonpost.com/wp-dyn/content/article/2009/07/09/AR2009070902391.html.

14. Ibid.

15. Ibid.

16. Gabriel Debendetti, "At Princeton, Sotomayor '76 Excelled at Academics, Extracurriculars," *The Daily Princetonian*, May 13, 2009, http://www.dailyprincetonian.com/2009/05/13/23695/.

17. Jason Michael Ferreira, "Student Movements—New Student Organizations, Continuing Organization, New York Times, Educational Opportunity Program, Puerto Ricans for Educational Progress," http://www.jrank.org/cultures/pages/4473/Student-Movements.html.

18. Ibid.

19. Winn, "Mentor at Princeton Recalls Sotomayor's Evolution."

20. Debendetti, "At Princeton, Sotomayor '76 Excelled at Academics, Extracurriculars."

21. Sonia Sotomayor, "Letter to the Editor," *Daily Princetonian*, May 10, 1974, http://www.dailyprincetonian.com/2009/05/15/23731/.

22. Debendetti, "At Princeton, Sotomayor '76 Excelled at Academics, Extracurriculars."

23. Winn, "Mentor at Princeton Recalls Sotomayor's Evolution."

24. Ibid.

25. Felix, *Sonia Sotomayor*, p. 51.

26. Winn, "Mentor at Princeton Recalls Sotomayor's Evolution."

Chapter 4

YALE LAW SCHOOL

The first year students in the law school class of '79 tended to keep to themselves, rarely raising their hands in class. Nervous about their studies, intimidated by professors and other law students, the first year students, often as not, spent their time complaining about their situation. The only student who did not seem fazed by her environment was Sonia Sotomayor, fresh from Princeton. "She was always willing to speak up and give her point of view," said classmate Robert Klonoff, now dean of the Lewis and Clark Law School in Portland, Oregon. "I just remember, even back then, thinking that in a group of very, very smart people she was destined to go great places."[1]

SEEKING DIRECTION

During her last semester at Princeton, Sotomayor made a trip to New Haven, Connecticut to visit Yale University. She was traveling with a friend who had an appointment with José Cabranes, a Puerto Rican lawyer who had recently taken on the job as the university's general counsel. Sotomayor's friend wished to talk to Cabranes about Puerto Rico's political history, as Cabranes had served as head of the

Commonwealth of Puerto Rico's office in Washington, D.C., as well as legal counsel to the governor of Puerto Rico.[2]

When the two arrived for their meeting with Cabranes, Sotomayor quickly engaged in an animated and spirited discussion of Puerto Rico's politics with the lawyer. The discussion outlasted the lunchtime appointment and stretched out for almost three hours. Cabranes was already aware of Sotomayor; a Princeton professor had told him about her sharp mind and engaging personality. It turned out that the two shared somewhat similar backgrounds; Cabranes was from Mayaguez, an area where Sotomayor had spent time when visiting family relatives in Puerto Rico. Cabranes had also grown up in the Bronx.[3]

During the meeting, Cabranes discussed with Sotomayor about a project he was working about the history of Puerto Rico. He promised to hire her as a summer research assistant after she completed her first year of law school. The meeting had a tremendous impact on Sotomayor; not only was Cabranes a well-respected Yale professor, but he was also the most prominent Puerto Rican attorney in the country. He would have tremendous influence on Sotomayor during her time at Yale.

WEDDING

In the midst of graduating from Princeton and preparing to attend law school was Sotomayor's wedding to her high-school sweetheart, Kevin Noonan. The couple wed on August 14, 1976, at St. Patrick's Cathedral in New York City. The church was the most prestigious Roman Catholic Church in New York City and one of the most well-known churches in the world. Sotomayor took her husband's last name and in the traditional Spanish way, was known as Sonia Sotomayor de Noonan.

The couple had little time afterwards to relax. Come September, Sotomayor was off to Yale to begin her classes, while Noonan attended Princeton to pursue his Ph.D. in molecular biology. The couple would do their best to balance their academic and personal lives in a long-distance relationship. While at law school, Sotomayor would earn the nickname, S.S. de Noonan, according to classmates, which was a play on her married name, while also suggesting the new bride as a formidable and forward moving ship.[4]

YALE LAW SCHOOL

Once again, Sotomayor found herself on the campus of one of the oldest educational institutions in the United States. Yale Law School originated in the office of a New Haven lawyer, Seth Staples. During the 18th and 19th centuries, many law students learned the finer points of their career by clerking as an apprentice in a lawyer's office. The first law schools, including the one that became Yale, developed out of this apprenticeship system and grew up inside law offices.[5]

In the case of Seth Staples, himself a graduate of Yale in the class of 1797, an outstanding library (an attraction for students at a time when law books were scarce) drew many law students to his office. Staples then decided to begin training apprentices in the early 1800s. By 1810, Staples's office had become a full-fledged law school. One of his students, Samuel Hitchcock, later became a partner at the office and then the proprietor of the New Haven Law School.[6]

Beginning in the 1820s, Staples and Hitchcock's New Haven Law School began its affiliation with Yale. In 1824, David Daggett, a former U.S. senator from Connecticut, joined Hitchcock as coproprietor of the school. Two years later in 1826, Yale named Daggett to be professor of law in Yale College, where he lectured to undergraduates on public law and government. This relationship continued until 1843, when law students began receiving law degrees from Yale. Yet, the school struggled for decades; with the death of Hitchcock in 1845 and his successor, Henry Dutton, in 1869, the University came near to closing the law school.[7]

AN ENDURING VISION

By the late 19th century, Yale Law School appeared to become a more viable resource as the university began to realize the importance of a legal education. It was during this period that the law school began to articulate two characteristics that have since become identified with the Yale Law School: first that the school would be "small and humane" in that the school would resist the temptation of large enrollments and impersonal relations between teachers and students like larger universities, and second, that the school would take an interdisciplinary approach to teaching the law.[8]

In order for this novel approach to succeed, the school established relationships with other departments, by asking members to teach classes at the law school. By the beginning of the 20th century, Yale created appointments of various faculty members that spanned everything from economics to psychiatry. In adopting this approach, Yale Law School directed the school and its students away from the preoccupation with private law practice that then typified American legal education. Instead its faculty and students engaged in more serious legal approaches toward public and international law.[9]

This resurrection of the law school would not have happened if not for the efforts of its first full-time dean, Francis Wayland. Wayland helped the school create a strong philanthropic base, which included the organization of the law library and the beginning of the prestigious legal periodical the *Yale Law Journal*. In addition, Yale pioneered a graduate program in law with the degree of Master of Laws being offered for the first time in 1876. By the beginning of the 20th century the Yale Law School acquired a reputation as a challenging and dynamic center of legal scholarship.[10]

In the 1930s, Yale Law School broke more new legal ground with the movement known as legal realism. This approach to the legal system helped reshape and redefine the way American lawyers understood the function of legal rules and the work of courts and judges. The movement emphasized paying attention to those factors that were not part of established legal rules. This might include things such as the attitudes of judges and the jurors to how facts in cases were interpreted. Under the influence of legal realism, American legal doctrine became less conceptual and more empirical. Building on this doctrine, the school also laid claim to a faculty that included some of the sharpest legal minds in the country at that time such as Thurman Arnold, Edwin Borchard, future U.S. Supreme Court Justice William O. Douglas, Jerome Frank, Underhill Moore, Walton Hamilton, and Wesley Sturges. The school also became known for the creation of the Federal Rules of Civil Procedure, which has been cited as the foundation of modern American procedure.[11]

During the 20th century, Yale Law graduates, because of their training, were in a unique position to play significant roles in international affairs and the domestic civil rights movement. During the 1950s and

1960s, the school also became a center of constitutional law, taxation, commercial law, international law, antitrust, and law and economics. In recent decades, the school then developed new courses in fields such as comparative constitutional law, corporate finance, environmental law, gender studies, international human rights, and legal history.[12]

LAW STUDIES

During her time at Yale, Sotomayor spent many hours in the Sterling Law Building, a large Gothic-Revival styled building, modeled after the noted English College, King's College located in Cambridge and, which occupied the better part of a city block. The library boasted a collection of no less than one million books; its space was dominated by high ceilings, large hanging lamps, and long study tables.[13]

As was the standard practice at the law school, Sotomayor and others in her class were split into small groups of 12 to 15 people. Each group attended the same classes, which were ungraded and instead relied on a pass/fail system of grading a student's abilities. The idea behind the simpler grading system was to foster a spirit of cooperation among students, rather than competition for high grades. One of Sotomayor's classmates stated that the nice thing about Yale was that "a great deal of effort is made to make it not a competitive experience. . . . Our torts professor, Guido Calabresi, gave us a little speech in our first semester, 'You're all going to pass, help each other.' That set the tone."[14]

Sotomayor's group proved quite amiable and soon, strong bonds among the students were formed. It was much easier to navigate the waters of first year law classes as a group than as one individual, like Sotomayor did in her early days at Princeton. The group took four classes the first semester; three of the courses were large classes that included other groups. The remaining class was a seminar taught by their small-group professor, Edward Dauer, a lawyer who also held graduate degrees in public health and health policy management. Dauer's specialty was the legal issues involving preventative healthcare, and viewed the law in terms of its economic impact and how it related to economic decisions.[15]

Their torts class was taught by Guido Calabresi, who helped found the school's law and economics movement. Students praised him for his "humanistic introduction" to the study of law as well as his warm and outgoing personality. Calabresi also emphasized the positive aspects of law school, wanting his students to learn in an atmosphere that was encouraging and challenging. Constitutional law was taught by Ralph K. Winter, who was an expert in antitrust law. The class's civil procedure course was taught by legal ethics expert Geoffrey Hazard, who was known for asking his students tough open-ended legal questions. However, Hazard's class with its terror-stricken students and tense atmosphere was the exception at Yale.[16]

FINDING HER PLACE

Once again, Sotomayor struggled with feelings of being out-of-place and intimidation at Yale, just as she had at Princeton. Even remembering her great successes at Princeton did not seem to help much. As she recalled later, "Nothing could prepare a kid from the South Bronx for the extraordinary power and prestige of Yale. Yale Law School students . . . are a different breed of smart and accomplishment; many of them do not even know they talk, think and live a totally different language and life than the rest of the world."[17]

Like Princeton, it would not be until almost her second year at school that Sotomayor began to take chances in class. She described her first time raising her hand in a class during a 1996 talk:

> I never raised my hands in my first-year classes at Yale. I was too embarrassed and too intimidated to ask questions. Only in my second year, in a Trusts and Estates class, did I finally raise my hand and give an answer in class. When Professor Clarke paused and looked at me and said that I had made an observation about the Rule against Perpetuities that he had never considered and that changed the answer to the example he was demonstrating, I felt like a million dollars.[18]

Sotomayor may not have been the smartest student in the class, but more importantly, she recognized then that there was a place for her among the students at Yale Law School.

Like her time at Princeton, Sotomayor made an impression on her classmates. One described her as being "tough, clear, very quick on her feet." Other former classmates categorized Sotomayor as being an "intellectually curious person, though sometimes quietly so." She was not one to command the spotlight, but she was involved. And while it was clear that she was bright, she was not a star. "She seemed to fit in with everybody. . . . Yale Law School typically has students that are very competitive, but she was loved by everyone." Another classmate remembered that Sotomayor "had an opinion, but she wasn't someone who talked a lot just to make people think she was smart."[19]

Classmates were also struck by her determination and strong work ethic. "At a time when other students were sitting around worrying about workload, she was doing the work," said Stephen Carter, who attended Yale Law School with Sotomayor and now is a professor there. Sotomayor also did not use her background as a means of qualifying herself in arguments. Carter remembers, "She would never sit around and say, 'Oh, well, I grew up in a housing project so I know. . . . She didn't feel her background gave her some kind of special trump. She wanted the argument to work. She would tell you why she thought something, and the 'why' never had anything to do with where she came from."[20]

OUTSIDE TIME

While at Yale, Sotomayor found ways to break away from the elite environment. Rudolph Aragon, who became a close friend of Sotomayor's while at Yale, remembered how "She felt an affinity with the African-American janitor, the workers, people in the cafeteria . . . There were so few minority students that we had to combine forces." In fact, the two would later create and cochair the Latin, Asian and Native American Association, an organization for minorities. Her closest friends at the school were also outsiders including Aragon who is Mexican American, along with three other students—a fellow Puerto Rican, a Mohawk Indian, and an African American.[21]

Aragon also remembered that Sotomayor "didn't just hang around the study carrel," and the two often met at each other's apartments to watch baseball games (Sotomayor was, and remains, a passionate New York Yankees fan). Aragon remembers how excited Sotomayor was during the 1977 World Series when the Yankees won. Sometimes Sotomayor and her friends would go to a local club to dance and drink beer. According to Aragon, she danced a "mean salsa."[22]

When not studying or spending downtime, Sotomayor was working. Even though she was going to Yale on a scholarship, she also worked a number of different jobs during her time there to make extra money. The summer she married, she spent working as a clerk at the Equitable Life Assurance Society of the United States in New York City. The summer after her first year at law school, Professor Cabranes came through on his promise to hire her as a research assistant. During her second year of school, Sotomayor worked at the Graduate and Professional Student Center on the Yale Campus; that summer she spent as

Sotomayor acknowledges the crowd as she's escorted by New York Yankees catcher Jorge Posada, left, to throw the ceremonial first pitch on the field before the New York Yankees vs. Boston Red Sox baseball game at Yankee Stadium, New York, September 26, 2009. (AP Photo/Bill Kostroun, FILE)

an associate at the law firm of Paul, Weiss, Rifkind, Wharton & Garrison in New York City. She spent her last year of law school working at the counter at the school's mimeo room where copies of various school documents were generated.[23]

Still, Sotomayor stood apart from her colleagues; some thought it was because she was married, others because of her background. Even when she was having fun, it was clear that Sotomayor intended to make the most of her time at Yale. She already knew what she wanted to do after graduating, which was to be a litigator or a lawyer who fights a lawsuit on behalf of his or her client in court.[24]

"TWICE AS GOOD"

During her time at Yale, Sotomayor recognized, along with many of the other minority students that even though they appeared to be fitting in with their classes and outside activities, they believed they had to "be twice as good and work twice as hard," in order to be accepted by their peers. Still no one was prepared for an event that shocked the Yale community and also showed white students that minority students faced a number of difficult challenges and pressures whether in the classroom or out in the world beyond.[25]

On October 2, 1978, Sotomayor, along with a group of other Yale law students, attended a recruiting dinner sponsored by a large Washington law firm, Shaw, Pittman, Potts & Trowbridge. The dinner was an opportunity for students to meet with the firm's members in advance of the more formal job interviews to take place the next day. During the dinner, a partner in the firm, Martin Krall, asked Sotomayor a number of questions that she was to discuss with him the following day during her interview. The questions consisted of the following:

- Do law firms do a disservice by hiring minority students who the firms know do not have the necessary credentials and will then fire in three to four years?
- Would I [Sotomayor] have been admitted to the law school if she were not a Puerto Rican?
- Was she culturally deprived?"

The next day, Sotomayor challenged Krall during her formal interview over the discriminatory nature of the questions. Krall told her
he meant nothing offensive by it and did not pursue it any further; he
even invited Sotomayor to come to Washington for further interviews
by the firm.[26]

Krall clearly thought the matter was a passing one and did not give
it any more thought. But Sotomayor refused to forget the incident.
Realizing that she was jeopardizing her future as a lawyer, much less
her opportunity to work with Shaw, Pittman, Potts & Trowbridge, she
decided to file a formal complaint against the law firm charging it with
discrimination and asking Yale to bar the firm from recruiting on campus. News of Sotomayor's actions spread through campus quickly and
within days, the incident had almost polarized the campus. Many of
her friends praised her for taking a stand, while others believed that
Sotomayor had gone too far.[27]

The debate raged across the campus; letters and petitions were
posted on bulletin boards either supporting or criticizing Sotomayor.
In addition, Yale's Black Student Union, the Latin, Asian and Native
American association, and Yale Law Women joined together in their
support of Sotomayor. It also came to light, that three recent Yale graduates working at Shaw, Pittman, Potts & Trowbridge were chastised by
Yale's Associate Dean James W. Zirkle for attempting to influence the
student-faculty tribunal who was asked to rule on Sotomayor's actions.
In the end, the tribunal found the complaint warranted and ordered
the law firm to write Sotomayor a letter of apology.[28]

As further evidence of the tribunal's support for Sotomayor, it rejected the law firm's initial letter of apology as "the firm did not seem
fully to recognize the consequences of its partner's action." Refusal to
address this issue held high consequences for Shaw, Pittman, Potts &
Trowbridge; if they did not present a satisfactory new letter, the firm
would be barred from recruiting at Yale. In the end, the firm did send
a letter of apology that was accepted. Still, the episode rocked the
50-lawyer firm, which included a large number of Yale graduates among
its partners and associates. These charges, which marred the reputation
of the firm, sent a strong message to other law schools in the country.[29]

Many of Sotomayor's friends applauded her controversial stand.
One friend, Robert Klonoff, who had been considering Shaw, Pittman,

Potts & Trowbridge as a possible employer scratched the firm from his potential employers list. He found the questions posed by the firm "ludicrous to ask someone who was a summa cum laude from Princeton. Nobody at law school thought that about her. She was eminently qualified, so smart." Klonoff also admired his friend's courage for standing up and challenging the firm: "Some people might have just buried the incident and not made a big issue of it. Some would not have wanted to attract attention, thinking it may be hard to get a job somewhere else. But she was not intimidated by that at all."[30]

If nothing else came out of the incident, many of Sotomayor's classmates became more aware of discriminatory practices and the seemingly innocent guise they can take. Robert Klonoff spoke for many when he said, "Having a classmate like her made me understand how evil racism is. It was one of a handful of signature events that I look back on now." One of Sotomayor's professors, Guido Calabresi saw the makings of a fine lawyer in the incident. He stated, "The way that Sonia has always stood up for these positions have in ways powerful, but friendly, and without that personal edge that says 'I've been hurt, I need revenge,' or something of that sort."[31]

LAW REVIEW

Sotomayor's final semester at Yale was packed; not only did she have her regular course studies to prepare for, she also learned that she was of 54 students picked as editors for the *Yale Law Journal*. Sotomayor earned her membership for her note, "Statehood and the Equal Footing Doctrine: The Case for Puerto Rico Seabed Rights." Her presentation earned her high marks from both student and faculty on the editorial board, and her acceptance of her work stood as one of the best decisions of the journal, which was known for its strong competitive edge.[32]

In her note, Sotomayor analyzed the possible hidden constitutional issues that would determine whether Puerto Rico would be allowed to maintain access to its seabed if it became a state. Sotomayor argued that if Puerto Rico was granted statehood, it should include in its agreement with the United States a clause that grants land rights to the ground in the ocean beyond that standard three-mile nautical limit. Extending this boundary would open up possible opportunities in recovering potential mineral and oil revenues, which would be of great boon to Puerto Rico. As Sotomayor stated, these revenues would be a necessity for a new state that suffered from a lack of land-based resources coupled with chronic economic stagnation and poverty.[33]

The note was an expansion of the research she had worked on as Professor Cabranes's research assistant during first semester as a law student. The direction of the note also built on her studies at Princeton and showed Sotomayor as being pro-independence on the issue of statehood for Puerto Rico. Stephen L. Carter, a classmate who helped Sotomayor edit her submission to the law journal remembers how even when she described positions which she disagreed, she was scrupulous about describing the argument as accurately as possible. Further, Sotomayor's work was fueled by a deep social worry about Puerto Rico and its future place in the world marketplace. Edward Rubin, another editor at the journal described her work as scholarly and balanced, given Sotomayor's own personal connection to Puerto Rico. Classmates remember just how hard she worked on it, polishing and repolishing it again.[34]

In addition to her studies and work at the journal, Sotomayor also served as managing editor of the *Yale Studies in World Public Order*, a secondary law journal founded by students in 1974. The journal provided a forum for scholarship and discussion in international law, a field that had been largely overlooked by other law journals at that time. Among her duties at that periodical were editing, proofreading, and fact-checking the submissions that were sent in. Even with all of those duties, Sotomayor still found time to participate in the annual Thomas Swan Barristers' Union mock trial competition, in which she advanced to the semifinals.[35]

By the spring of 1979, Sotomayor also began thinking about preparing for the bar exam that was to be offered in July. Several of her classmates began studying together in the hope of passing and then moving on to jobs by the fall. Many of her classmates studying for the bar exam were using the BAR/BRI study course, which was designed specifically to cover multistate section of the bar exam. Instead, Sotomayor and her friends opted for the PLI or Practicing Law Institute study course because it cost less than the BAR/BRI course. Sotomayor was even able to get her fee waived when she agreed to be the campus representative for the PLI review course. She also helped to put together the schedule for the class that was anywhere from 8 to 10 weeks, ordered the necessary materials, and set up the tapes that the students would listen to. Because Sotomayor and several of her classmates hoped to practice in New York, they made sure their review course included the New York state portion of the exam.[36]

Graduation came and went. Sotomayor and her friends barely celebrated, instead keeping their heads down as they prepared to take the July exam, which was six hours long and contained 200 multiple choice questions. Preparing for the exam basically meant hours and hours of listening to tapes and memorizing the necessary information. Sotomayor and four of her friends met every day at school in a room where they sat and listened for hours to the review tapes. As one of her classmates stated later, "We were miserable." But the misery and long hours paid off. Everybody passed the exam. It was the end of another long and hard road for Sotomayor. But she had passed, not only in her studies, but in taking on issues that were of concern to her and felt passionately about. Now she was ready to leave the confines of the Ivy League campuses with their pristine campuses and elite atmospheres, and reenter the gritty urban world she had grown up in. She was going back to New York City.[37]

NOTES

1. Elizabeth Landau, "Sotomayor Always Willing to Speak Up at Yale Law," *CNNPolitics*, May 26, 2009, http://articles.cnn.com/2009–05–26/politics/sotomayor.princeton.yale_1_yale-law-school-class mates-sonia-sotomayor?_s=PM:POLITICS.

2. Antonia Felix, *Sonia Sotomayor: The True American Dream*, New York: Berkeley Publishing Group, 2010, p. 56.

3. Ibid., pp. 56–57.

4. Ibid., pp. 57–58; Zeke Miller, "At Yale Sotomayor was Sharp but Not Outspoken," *Yale Daily News*, May 31, 2009, http://www.yaledai lynews.com/news/2009/may/31/at-yale-sotomayor-was-sharp-but-not-outspoken/.

5. "History of YLS," http://www.law.yale.edu/about/historyofyls. htm#.

6. Ibid.

7. Ibid.

8. Ibid.

9. Ibid.

10. Ibid.

11. Ibid.

12. Ibid.

13. Felix, *Sonia Sotomayor*, p. 57.

14. Ibid.

15. Ibid., p. 58.

16. Ibid., p. 59.

17. Sonia Sotomayor, "The Genesis and Needs of an Ethnic Identity," November 7, 1996.

18. Ibid.

19. Sheryl Gay Stolberg, "Sotomayor, a Trailblazer and Dreamer," *New York Times*, May 26, 2009, http://www.nytimes.com/2009/05/27/us/politics/27websotomayor.html?pagewanted=all; Landau, "Sotomayor Always \ Willing to Speak Up at Yale Law."

20. Stolberg, "Sotomayor, a Trailblazer and Dreamer"; Landau, "Sotomayor Always Willing to Speak Up at Yale Law."

21. Stolberg, "Sotomayor, a Trailblazer and Dreamer."

22. Ibid.

23. Felix, *Sonia Sotomayor*, p. 62.

24. Stolberg, "Sotomayor, a Trailblazer and Dreamer."

25. Felix, *Sonia Sotomayor*, p. 62.

26. Ibid.; Stewart Auerbach, "Law Firm Apologizes to Yale Student," *Washington Post*, December 16, 1978, p. D3.

27. Auerbach, "Law Firm Apologizes to Yale Student."

28. Ibid.

29. Ibid.; James Oliphant and Andrew Zajac, "At Yale, Sotomayor Won Apology from Law Firm," *Los Angeles Times*, May 29, 2009, http://articles.latimes.com/2009/may/28/nation/na-sotomayor-apology28.

30. Felix, *Sonia Sotomayor*, p. 63.

31. Ibid., p. 64.

32. Ibid., pp. 64–65.

33. Ibid.

34. Ibid., p. 65.
35. Ibid., pp. 64–66.
36. Ibid., p. 66.
37. Ibid.

Chapter 5

NEW YORK DA

Throughout her last year at law school, Sotomayor thought about what she might want to do once she graduated. Like her classmates, Sotomayor had several interviews with law firms located in several large cities throughout the country. Sotomayor also placed an application with the State Department, thinking she might like to practice international law. But her real hope was to practice in New York City where she would be closer to her family and friends.

There was also the issue of her husband, Kevin, who had completed his studies at Princeton and was now looking into post-graduate programs. The good news was that Kevin also wanted to move back to New York City, so the two continued their job searches hoping that they both would find something exciting and filled with opportunity in their hometown.

MEETING MR. MORGENTHAU

One evening while Sotomayor was studying in the law library, she became hungry and set off to find something to eat and drink. She left the library and entered a third-floor conference room. That decision led her to more than just an evening meal. At an awards ceremony in 1995, Sotomayor described what happened next:

> Down the hall from the library I saw cheese and wine in the back of the third-floor conference room and that was more than enough to draw my attention. The assembled speakers in the room were public interest lawyers who were discussing the alternatives to private practice. I don't remember the other speakers because Bob Morgenthau—fortunately for me who was only there for the nutrients in the room—was the last speaker being introduced.
>
> After affirming the many benefits of public service . . . Bob described his office and its work. He indicated that a position with his office differed from almost all other public and private work because only in his office would you actually be trying a case within your first year and where you would have significant and ultimate responsibility in the development and presentation of your cases. At twenty-four/twenty-five years of age . . . you would do more in a courtroom than many lawyers did in a lifetime.[1]

Sotomayor soon realized that she was talking to one of the most influential and successful district attorneys (DAs) in the nation as well as one of New York City's most well-respected figures and power brokers.

At the time of their meeting, Robert Morgenthau had emerged as one New York City's most powerful attorneys. In the four years since he had come to New York City, Morgenthau, as the lead prosecutor for Manhattan, an office that many consider to be the premier prosecutor's office in the United States, had already carved a name for himself as a tough prosecutor, known for his dogged determination in prosecuting organized and white-collar criminals.[2]

Robert Morris Morgenthau was born in New York City on July 31, 1919, the son of a prominent Jewish family. The family was also well regarded in political circles; Morgenthau's father, Henry Morgenthau, served under Presidents Roosevelt and Truman as the Secretary of the Treasury, his grandfather, Henry Morgenthau Sr., served as ambassador to the Ottoman Empire under Woodrow Wilson. He remembers growing up and visiting the White House and playing on President Roosevelt's lap; Eleanor Roosevelt wrote to him while he was at the elite boarding school Exeter. He sailed boats with young John F. Kennedy. But Robert never felt any pressure from his famous father to go into politics. As he later recalled in an interview, "There was no expectation either way. At the age of 12 I wanted to either go to West Point or become a fireman."[3]

Morgenthau attended Amherst, and then joined the U.S. Navy where he served during World War II. After the war, he attended Yale Law School where he graduated in 1948. He then went into private practice and spent the next 13 years working as a white-collar litigator. In 1961, Morgenthau was appointed U.S. Attorney for the Southern District of New York, by his old childhood friend, President John F. Kennedy. For the next 9 years, as a U.S. attorney, Morgenthau established a special unit to investigate white-collar crimes such as securities fraud and pursued highly publicized and political bribery cases against city officials, IRS attorneys, and accountants. It was the beginning of a public service career that spanned almost five decades, three of them with the City of New York.[4]

In 1975, Morgenthau took office as the district attorney of New York County. In an interview with CNN, Morgenthau stated his dedication to public service was the result of a promise he made as a young Navy officer. In 1944, his ship, the USS Lansdale was torpedoed off the coast of Algiers. As the ship began to sink, Morgenthau vowed that if he survived he would dedicate his life to public service. "I'd always thought of going into government service," Morgenthau recalled. "But when my ship was torpedoed off Algiers and I was floating around in the water, I made promises to the Almighty."[5]

Some would say Morgenthau kept his promise as he set out to revamp the Manhattan district attorney's office into the nation's foremost prosecutor's office. Under his direction, the office grew to include 34 bureaus and units, specializing in everything from labor racketeering to street gangs to cold cases to elder abuse cases. Morgenthau also increased the sex crimes unit; his model was used as a prototype for similar units throughout the United States.[6]

JOB OFFER

Even though Sotomayor believed that she did not make a good first impression on Morgenthau, the fact was quite the opposite; the DA was very impressed with the engaging law student. In testimony given before the Senate committee hearings for Sotomayor's nomination to the Supreme Court, Morgenthau described how he decided to hire her:

> I first came to know Judge Sotomayor when I was on a recruiting trip for the Yale Law School. At that time, Jose Febrenes [*sic*] [Cabranes] was Yale's general counsel, and he also tailored the law school. I asked him if he knew anyone special I should speak with, and he said, yes. He said the remarkable student named Sonia Sotomayor was deciding where to work. And while he did not know whether she'd given any thought to being a prosecutor, it would be well worth my while to meet her. He was decidedly correct. I'm happy to be able to say that [she] joined my office.[7]

A few weeks after their talk and Morgenthau's discussion with Cabranes, Sotomayor came to New York City with a classmate to look over the offices of the Manhattan DA, located at Foley Square and to assess if this was the direction she wanted to pursue.

On the day of their visit, Morgenthau offered Sotomayor a job in his office. She agreed on one condition: her acceptance would depend on whether her husband was able to enter a graduate program of his choice in New York City. If Kevin was unable to do that, then Sotomayor would regretfully have to decline the DA's offer. It was a few months before everything fell into place. To Sotomayor's amazement and gratitude, Morgenthau had so much confidence in her abilities, that he kept the offer open. In August 1979, Sonia Sotomayor de Noonan began her tenure with the DA's office in New York City. It was a measure of how highly Morgenthau valued Sotomayor's talents and aptitude for the job.[8]

Sotomayor's decision to work for Morgenthau shocked her classmates. First, there was the issue of the lower pay one would earn working for the city as opposed to private practice and second, was Sotomayor's own passions for the pursuit of minority rights and diversity in everything from college campuses to the workplace. As she stated later in a newspaper article in 1983, "There was a tremendous amount of pressure from my community, from the third-world community, at

Yale. They could not understand why I was taking this job. I'm not sure I ever resolved that problem."[9]

Another reason to reconsider the job was the state of New York City itself. Throughout the 1970s, the city had earned itself a reputation for being one of the most troubled cities in America. The stagnating U.S. economy hit New York City particularly hard; the New York Stock Exchange suffered large losses and the city's spending on welfare increased. At one point, the city teetered on the edge of bankruptcy but was saved with the help of a large loan from the U.S. government. The city was falling down and falling apart: the subway system was regarded as unsafe due to crime and frequent mechanical breakdowns. The streets of Times Square, once noted as the agora of New York City because of its theaters, hotels, and other cultural draws, was now filled with more unsavory elements such as prostitutes and drug dealers; the theaters were replaced by sex shops and adult movie theaters. Central Park became feared as the site of muggings and rapes. In 1979, the city numbered almost 18 million residents. It also had one of the highest crime rates in the country; in 1979 alone, there 161,906 incidents of violent crime in New York including 2,092 murders, 5,394 rapes, 93,471 robberies, and 60,949 aggravated assaults. Car thefts were a staggering 124,343, while there were over 500,000 instances of larceny and theft.[10]

Despite the appalling statistics, and the low pay, to Sotomayor the job offered two important perks: real-life experience and the chance to try cases right away. Working for Morgenthau would place her in the front lines of one of the most challenging law offices in the world. Or as Morgenthau jokingly said in an interview: "I tell people, half-seriously, half-joking, that there are two main drawbacks to the office. One is that the salaries are not as good as private practice. (The average salary for an assistant District Attorney was $17,000.) The other is that they're going to like the job so much they're not going to want to leave."[11]

THE DA'S OFFICE

By the time Sotomayor went to work for the Manhattan DA's office, Morgenthau had been in charge for almost five years. During that period, a number of changes had taken place. Linda Fairstein, who began working in the office in 1972, was one of seven women hired out of a total pool of 180 attorneys. She remembers that initially women were discouraged from taking part in criminal trials because of the gruesome nature of the cases. The head of the DA Office at that time was a man by the name of Frank Hogan, who was an able prosecutor but very old fashioned. According to Fairstein, she was told by Hogan that criminal court work was too "tawdry" and instead pushed women to work in the law library or for the grand jury or appellate courts. After Hogan died, Morgenthau came—and with him a whole new way of running the DA's office. As Fairstein stated in a later interview, "[Morgenthau] had entirely different ideas—[and] was enormously progressive about diversity in every sense of the word."[12]

After a very brief training seminar, the new assistants found themselves not acting as attorneys in mock trials but doing the real thing with real cases, real criminals, and real victims. To begin with, junior DAs took on misdemeanor crimes such as shoplifting, misdemeanor assaults, prostitution, and petty larceny before they were given more difficult felony cases. Still, it was an intense introduction into the world of criminal law. Fortunately, Morgenthau also made sure that the new assistants were taken in hand by more experienced lawyers and when necessary, by the bureau chief and the deputy bureau chief. Every morning, Sotomayor, dressed in an inexpensive suit, would walk into the faded art deco building that houses the DA's office where she would work in a space that was originally designed to hold one person but was often crowded with three or four other prosecutors. Then there was the intake room, a space where criminal complaints were filed, that at any time was filled with police officers, attorneys, and crime victims. Metal desks throughout the office might be overflowing with papers and boxes of evidence. Early on though, Sotomayor strove to maintain organization and discipline in the midst of chaos; her desk was always the neatest one in the room.

As a new assistant, Sotomayor was assigned to Trial Bureau 50, a unit that consisted of more than two dozen prosecutors who handled everything from misdemeanors to felony murder. Marsha Papanek, a prosecutor, helped train Sotomayor described her as "really impressive" but who was also susceptible to an attack of nerves when the action started. "I just remember at that particular point," Ms. Papanek said, "she was like all the others that start: scared to death to go in front of a criminal court judge."[13]

For the first few months Sotomayor was in the office, she prosecuted cases that ranged from disorderly conduct, public urination, turnstile jumping to the defacing of public and private property by graffiti. Still in spite of her zeal to uphold the law, Sotomayor was also aware that a number of the crimes were committed because of other social ills: poverty, being the biggest. In a 1983 article on Morgehthau and the DA's office, Sotomayor stated, "I had more problems during my first year in the office with the low-grade crimes—the shoplifting, the prostitution, the minor assault cases . . . In large measure, in those cases you were dealing with socioeconomic crimes, crimes that could be the product of the environment and of poverty."[14]

At her confirmation hearings in 2009, Sotomayor credits Morgenthau with helping her become a lawyer. As she told the Senate committee:

I became a lawyer in the prosecutor's office. . . . When I say I became a lawyer in his office, it's because in law school—law schools teach you on hypotheticals. They set forth facts for you. They give you a little bit of teaching on how those facts are developed, but not a whole lot, and then they ask you to opine about legal theory and apply legal theory to the facts before you. Well, when you work in a prosecutor's office, you understand that the law is not legal theory, it's facts. It's what witnesses say and don't say. It's how you develop the—your position in the record. And then it's taking those facts and making arguments based on the law as it exists. . . . It is respect that each case gets decided case by case, applying the law as it exists to the facts before you.[15]

Within six months, she was promoted to handle more serious felonies, well ahead of her freshman class of prosecutors. Her colleagues were struck by her almost obsessive focus on the details of any given criminal case, spending hours studying the evidence as she put together her evidences and arguments. "She angsted over all her trial cases," Dawn Cardi, who worked with Sotomayor said in a 2009 interview. "She would sort of disappear into her work. You would have to remind her that she had to eat." Another colleague stated that Sotomayor "was driven. . . . Definitely, driven and serious and competitive."[16]

Cardi, who was working as a criminal defense lawyer was not long out of law school herself. She first met Sotomayor in 1980, when she went up against the tough, young assistant DA. The case that involved Cardi's client—a 20-something father who had hit a subway rider with his umbrella—did not go well and her client was now standing in front of the judge. Cardi was also worried that because of her inexperience her client would go to jail instead of receiving a stern lecture on his behavior.[17]

Much to Cardi's surprise, Sotomayor stood up and addressed the judge, asking that the judge give the accused probation instead. Cardi was stunned, knowing that a prosecutor's career was made for appearing tough and winning stiff sentences in criminal cases. In the end, Cardi invited Sotomayor out for lunch, and the two women became good friends. During Sotomayor's confirmation hearings Cardi recalled the incident saying that "A lot of district attorneys thought they were doing God's work. But she saw it as a civic responsibility. . . . She was also concerned that if there wasn't enough evidence, someone shouldn't be prosecuted."[18]

Sotomayor quickly earned a reputation as an extremely bright and driven prosecutor. Whether discussing points of law with lawyers or in front of a judge or interviewing a victim of a crime, Sotomayor's instincts were solid. "She had a foot in both worlds, and she was comfortable in both of those worlds," said Richard H. Girgenti, a former supervisor. Peter M. Kougasian, a former classmate of Sotomayor's at Yale who also worked at the DA's office described his friend as demonstrating a maturity not often seen among new assistant DA's. He later stated, "When you walk into a courtroom and say you represent the people of the State of New York, I think for her that was not just an abstraction. . . . She had experienced so many aspects of life that make up a great city, that when she said that, you had the feeling that she knew what she was talking about in a way that the rest of us maybe didn't."[19]

On average, prosecutors were expected to juggle 80 to 100 cases at a time; during her time in the DA's office Sotomayor tried approximately 20 cases before juries. To meet the ongoing demands and strains of the job, Sotomayor became a caffeine addict who started her day with a Tab, a popular diet drink; on average she drank almost 20 cans a day along with smoking close to a pack and a half of cigarettes. Her days began early in the morning, ended sometime close to midnight when Sotomayor would board the subway to her home in Brooklyn. Many nights Sotomayor often stopped by Dawn Cardi's brownstone for a quick dinner that might consist of pasta or pot roast and a glass of scotch. "My baby would be asleep, and we would sit down and chat about our lives," said Cardi, who was then working as a legal aid lawyer. The two women compared notes on their cases, amazed that "their lives seemed straight out of prime-time television, full of petty crooks, tough-talking judges and courtroom drama."[20]

But Sotomayor was also a realist when it came to her job. As she told a reporter to the *New York Times Magazine* in 1983:

> The one thing I have found is that if you come into the criminal justice system on a prosecutorial or defense level thinking that you can change the ills of society, you're going to be sorely disappointed. This is not where those kinds of changes have to be made. It pains me, when I meet particularly bright defendants— and I've met quite a few of them—people who, if they had had the right guidance, the right education, the right breaks, could have been contributing members of our society. When they get convicted, there's a satisfaction, because they're doing things that are dangerous. But there are also nights when I sit back and say, "My God, what a waste!"

One former colleague in the office said, "I think she wanted to make sure that her cases were solid and that she was dispensing justice before just locking someone up or putting them away, as opposed to being an overzealous prosecutor who believed that if you were arrested you were automatically guilty."[21]

"NO-NONSENSE"

During the 1970s, the use of children in pornography dramatically increased. As a result, by 1982, almost all of the states and the United States Congress passed laws banning child pornography. One of the first states to get a law on the books was New York, which, in 1977 created a law that made the use of children less than 16 years old in sexual or simulated sexual performances a felony. Further, the material did not have to fall under the legal definition of obscene, that is, considered as a whole to be offensive and lacking in serious value, to be prohibited.[22]

Soon after the law passed, undercover police officers in New York City arrested Paul Ferber, an adult bookstore owner. Ferber was accused of selling the officers two films containing sexually explicit footage of two underage boys. Even though a jury in New York's lower court did not find the films to be legally obscene, the jury did convict Ferber under the New York child Pornography Law. The case then traveled to the state Appellate Section of the New York Supreme Court who upheld the conviction. However, when the case reached the New York Court of Appeals, the conviction was reversed, stating that the material fell under the protection of the first amendment (freedom of speech) since the original jury did not find the material obscene. The court also ruled that nonobscene adolescent sex remained a too narrow form of speech to be excluded from First Amendment protection.[23]

Morgenthau then appealed the decision to the United States Supreme Court, which unanimously upheld the original convictions. Justice Byron White, writing for the court stated that:

> The distribution of photographs and films depicting sexual activity by juveniles is intrinsically related to the sexual abuse of children in at least two ways. First, the materials produced are a permanent record of the children's participation and the harm to the child is exacerbated by their circulation. Second, the distribution network for child pornography must be closed if the production of material which requires the sexual exploitation of children is to be effectively controlled.[24]

The court also noted that the state of New York had flexibility in how it regulated child pornography and that the law was valid.[25]

Within the year, Sotomayor would go to trial with the first case to be tried under the newly upheld child pornography law. The case began when former New York police detective Chris Montanino was trying to get someone in the DA's office to go after some child-porn distributors but was having a difficult time getting someone to work with him.

He came to his office and saw that he had a message to return a call to a young woman in the DA's office. When Montanino returned the call, he recalled, "I blew my top," complaining that his case, which consisted of a number of child pornography materials that he had purchased at a Manhattan bookstore, had done nothing but been passed around to different prosecutors. "This is baloney," he said to the voice on the telephone. As he was getting ready to continue his diatribe, he was cut off. "You will be in my office at 9 a.m. tomorrow," the voice said before hanging up on him. "And that is the way it went," Montanino later said in an interview. "[Sotomayor] was no-nonsense."[26]

The case proved to be a difficult and emotional one. Montanino remembers Sotomayor as being determined and stoic, even as she watched grainy black and white films showing children aged 7 to 14 engaged in sex acts. By the time the case came to trial, Sotomayor's excellent prosecution that included showing excerpts of the films in question left many jurors crying.

The outcome proved to be another important victory for Sotomayor and the DA's office as the store owner and clerk were found guilty and sentenced to prison terms. As one onlooker commented about Sotomayor, "She isn't someone who lived her life in some ivory tower. . . . She is somebody who grew up in the projects; she prosecuted cases that came from those areas, she saw how those cases devastated the victims. That informs her judgment." The case was also important in that it was the first child pornography case prosecuted in New York after the landmark 1982 Supreme Court decision, *People v. Ferber*, upholding New York's new child pornography laws.[27]

TARZAN MURDERS

One of the most high-profile cases handled by the DA's office would also land in Sotomayor's lap in 1982. Over the course of three months, a violent crime spree had held Harlem in a chilling grip of terror. Between 1981 and 1982, a criminal known as the Tarzan burglar had been terrorizing residents by breaking into apartments. But it was not just the fact that he broke into apartments; it was the way he did it: by swinging on a rope and crashing through the windows. In some cases, the intruder just robbed the apartments. But other times he had smashed through the windows, firing his gun. "He was fearless," said Hugh H.

Mo, who would be the lead prosecutor on the case. "If he found people, he would just blast away."[28]

By the time police caught up with the suspect he had broken into more than 20 residences, injured half a dozen people, and had murdered three people. All the crimes had been committed within 11 blocks of each other. Detectives from Harlem's 28th Precinct and the Manhattan Detective Task Force investigated the crimes for over two months. Finally, on January 28, 1982, detectives arrested a 37-year-old drug addict, Richard Maddicks, who at the time of his arrest was carrying a .32 revolver. Police then searched Maddicks's girlfriend's apartment where they found more evidence of the robberies and murders that definitively linked Maddicks to the crimes. He was arrested and charged.[29]

Hugh H. Mo, who would work with Sotomayor on prosecuting Maddicks remembers the high-profile nature of the case. According to him, the case had a little bit of everything: "murder, assault, burglary, weapons possession. . . . It was a prosecutor's dream." For Sotomayor, the case was unlike anything she had dealt with before. Because Maddicks had committed so many separate crimes over a two-year period, "it was like seven trials put into one," Mo later recounted.[30]

It was also Sotomayor's first murder case, and like any other case, she threw everything she had into putting together the best case she could. "She had that uncanny ability of putting together a complicated set of facts and distilling them into a very simple story that would resonate with the jury," Mo said. "That's unusual for a young attorney." Sotomayor also catalogued evidence, interviewed witnesses, and visited crime scenes. At one point, she and Mo accompanied New York detectives into a vacant building often frequented by drug addicts. "I took a deep breath, and Sonia took a deep breath," Mo said. "Here we were, trained trial lawyers in the field hunting down a witness. It was a searing experience."[31]

The prosecutor's office had a challenge in front of them: how best to present Maddicks actions to a jury. As Sotomayor explained during her confirmation hearings, there was a great deal at stake:

> At the same time, as a prosecutor in that case, I had to consider how to ensure that the presentation of that case would be fully understood by jurors. And to do that, it was important for us as prosecutors to be able to present those number of incidences that

Mr. Maddicks had engaged in, in one trial, so the full extent of his conduct could be determined by a jury. There had never been a case quite like that, where an individual who used different ac-robatic feats to gain entry into an apartment was tried with all of his crimes in one indictment. I researched very carefully the law and found a theory in New York law, called the Molineux theory then, that basically said if you can show a pattern that established a person's identity or assisted in establishing a person's identity—simplifying the argument, by the way—then you can try different cases together. This was not a conspiracy, under law, because Mr. Maddicks acted alone, so I had to find a different theory to bring all his acts together.[32]

Sotomayor and Mo were able to convince a judge that Maddicks' ac-tions fell under the Molineux theory, allowing them to try Maddicks in a joint trial for all of his crimes.[33]

Mo had so much confidence in his assistant that he even let Soto-mayor present a portion of the Tarzan murder case in court, something that is not often done with assistant DAs. Mo said that Sotomayor helped convince Maddicks's girlfriend to testify for the prosecution, and that once the trial started her dexterity was impressive. With one witness, she could patiently draw out the details of the drug trade. With another, the sister of one of the murder victims, she used a softer touch. "She was able to gently bring out the loss she observed, the trauma she suffered," Mo said. After nearly a month of testimony, the jury found Maddicks guilty and sentenced him to 67½ years to life in prison. Afterward, Sotomayor and Mo went out and celebrated the victory.[34]

PARTING

Sotomayor's year had been marked by two high-profile court cases that ended in convictions by the DA's office. She had shown herself to be meticulous in putting together her cases, dogged in tracking down pieces of evidence and talking to witnesses, fearless in the courtroom, yet possessing a gentle touch when needed in talking to victims and their families. As Morgenthau stated at her confirmation hearings in 2009, Sotomayor "understood that every case is important to the victim and appropriately gave undivided attention to the proper disposition of all of them."[35]

But Sotomayor's determination and commitment to her work ultimately came at a high price. Her marriage to her high-school sweetheart, Kevin Noonan, broke up. For months, the couple's lives had grown increasingly divergent. By now Noonan had completed his PhD and was on his way to Chicago to attend law school. Sotomayor's long hours at the DA's office had not helped either. Sotomayor later admitted that while her long work hours was not the sole reason for the divorce, it did not help her marriage and if anything, made it more difficult to realize that there were problems. Still, the parting was amicable, as both Sotomayor and Noonan realized that they had grown apart. As one of Sotomayor's colleagues commented, "They weren't the same people as when they got married. It was kind of like, 'Let's divide up the milk crates where we stored the books.'"[36]

The couple's divorce was finalized in October; Sotomayor returned to her maiden name, moved to an apartment in Brooklyn and moved on with her life. She marked the new transition in her life with a get-together of her friends at her new home. She was not bitter over her divorce, nor did she feel rancor toward her former husband. If anything, she cautioned her colleagues in the office such as Hugh Mo to be mindful of working long and late hours because of the stress it placed on marriage and family life.[37]

NEW DIRECTIONS

In the spring of 1984, Sonia Sotomayor left the prosecutor's office, opting to go into private practice. Dawn Cardi firmly believes that Sotomayor's time in the DA's office was pivotal for her and helped shape her future direction as a lawyer. "She was a far better litigator . . . she could take over a courtroom," Cardi said. "She saw the impact that crime had on our society . . . she thought a lot about how we address it. . . . As you get older and more experienced, it gets more complicated. You see shades of gray. I think she began to see these were complicated cases, they are not as simple as crime and punishment."[38]

Sotomayor would be deeply grateful to Morgenthau for the opportunity to work under him. "I don't know how he saw the chord in me that responded so strongly to trial work." She said later. "I loved litigating, I loved being a prosecutor. It was [wonderful] and enormously gratifying work that I enjoyed tremendously. Most of all, however, I loved being in an office surrounded by people whose values I respected and who taught me so many important lessons."[39]

For Sotomayor, the journey so far had a strange, but logical progression: from her early reading of the Nancy Drew mysteries to her faithful watching of the *Perry Mason* television show, to law school to Morgenthau's office. In a later speech, she remembered a particular episode from the program that defined for her what the law and a lawyer's job was all about:

> I may have been the only fan of the show who liked the ever-losing prosecutor, [Hamilton] Berger. My like for him developed from one episode in which Perry Mason expressed sympathy for the frustration Berger had to be feeling after working so hard on his case and having it dismissed. Berger responded by observing that as a prosecutor his job was to find the truth and that if the truth led to the acquittal of the innocent and the dismissal of his case, then he had done his job right and justice had been served. His speech stayed with me my entire life and shaped my perception of what prosecutors did.[40]

What Sotomayor also took from her five years working in the DA's office was the experience that comes from working in the trenches as it were, applying the law, and learning the law. That experience became one of the most important and defining signatures to her life and that would make her nomination in 2009 different from most nominees to the Supreme Court.

NOTES

1. Sonia Sotomayor, "Remarks on Receiving the Hogan-Morgenthau Award," New York City, January 17, 1995.

2. Carlin DeGuerin Miller, "Real Life 'Law & Order' DA Robert Morgenthau Retires at 90," *CBS News*, December 31, 2009, http://www.cbsnews.com/8301–504083_162–6041975–504083.html.

3. Robert Kolker, "Happy 85th Birthday Bob Morgenthau," *New York Magazine*, May 25, 2005, http://nymag.com/nymetro/news/politics/newyork/features/9546/; Corey M. Baker, "Robert Morgenthau," *Jewish Virtual Library*, http://www.jewishvirtuallibrary.org/jsource/biography/RobertMorgenthau.html.

4. Kolker, "Happy 85th Birthday Bob Morgenthau."

5. Ibid.

6. Miller, "Real Life 'Law & Order' DA Robert Morgenthau Retires at 90."

7. "District Attorney of New York County Robert Morgenthau Testifies at Judge Sotomayor's Confirmation Hearings," *Washington Post*, July 16, 2009, http://www.washingtonpost.com/wp-dyn/content/article/2009/07/16/AR2009071602990.html.

8. Sotomayor, "Remarks on Receiving the Hogan-Morgenthau Award."

9. Jonathan Barzilay, "The D.A.'s Right Arms," *New York Times Magazine*, November 23, 1983, p. 118.

10. "New York Crime Rates 1960–2009," http://www.disastercenter.com/crime/nycrime.htm.

11. Barzilay, "The D.A.'s Right Arms."

12. Charisse Dengler, "Linda Fairstein: Author and Former Head of the Manhattan District Attorney's Office's Sex Crimes Unit," *LawCrossing*, http://www.lawcrossing.com/article/2403/Linda-Fairstein-Author-and-Former-Head-of-the-Manhattan-District-Attorney-s-Office-s-Sex-Crimes-Unit/.

13. Benjamin Weister and William K. Rashbaum, "Sotomayor Is Recalled as a Driven Rookie Prosecutor," *New York Times*, June 8, 2009, Section A, p. 13.

14. Barzilay, "The D.A.'s Right Arms."

15. "Sotomayor Confirmation Hearings Day 2," *New York Times*, July 14, 2009, http://www.nytimes.com/2009/07/14/us/politics/14confirm-text.html?pagewanted=all.

16. Joe Stephens and Del Quentin Wilber, "Gritty First Job Shaped Nominee," *Washington Post*, June 4, 2009, p. A01.

17. Ibid.

18. Ibid.

19. Weister and Rashbaum, "Sotomayor Is Recalled as a Driven Rookie Prosecutor."

20. Stephens and Wilber, "Gritty First Job Shaped Nominee."

21. Barzilay, "The D.A.'s Right Arms."; Weister and Rashbaum, "Sotomayor is Recalled as a Driven Rookie Prosecutor."

22. "*New York v. Ferber*: Significance," *LawJrank*, http://law.jrank. org/pages/23393/New-York-v-Ferber-Significance.html.

23. Ibid.

24. Byron White, "Opinion of the Court, Supreme Court of the United States, 458 U.S. 747, *New York v. Ferber*," http://www.law. cornell.edu/supct/html/historics/USSC_CR_0458_0747_ZO.html.

25. "*New York v. Ferber*: Significance."

26. Dina Temple-Raston, "Sotomayor's Real-World Schooling in Law and Order," *NPR*, http://www.npr.org/templates/story/story.php? storyId=105005007.

27. Ibid.

28. Weister and Rashbaum, "Sotomayor Is Recalled as a Driven Rookie Prosecutor."

29. Antonia Felix, *Sonia Sotomayor: The True American Dream*, New York: Berkeley Publishing Group, 2010, p. 94.

30. Weister and Rashbaum, "Sotomayor Is Recalled as a Driven Rookie Prosecutor."

31. James Oliphant, "Sotomayor Remembered as Zealous Prosecutor," *Los Angeles Times*, June 9, 2009, http://articles.latimes.com/2009/ jun/09/nation/na-sotomayor-prosecutor9.

32. Temple-Raston, "Sotomayor's Real-World Schooling in Law and Order."

33. "Sotomayor Confirmation Hearings Day 2," *The New York Times*, July 14, 2009, http://www.nytimes.com/2009/07/14/us/politics/14confirm-text.html?pagewanted=all.

34. Oliphant, "Sotomayor Remembered as Zealous Prosecutor."

35. "District Attorney of New York County Robert Morgenthau Testifies at Judge Sotomayor's Confirmation Hearings," *Washington Post*, July 16, 2009, http://www.washingtonpost.com/wp-dyn/content/ article/2009/07/16/AR2009071602990.html.

36. Michael Powell, Serge F. Kovaleski and Russ Buettner, "To Get to Sotomayor's Core, Start in New York," *New York Times*, July 9, 2009, http:// www.nytimes.com/2009/07/10/nyregion/10sonia.html?pagewanted=all.

37. Felix, *Sonia Sotomayor*, pp. 110–11.

38. Temple-Raston, "Sotomayor's Real-World Schooling in Law and Order."

39. Sotomayor, "Remarks on Receiving the Hogan-Morgenthau Award."

40. Ibid.

Chapter 6

PRIVATE PRACTICE

At a going away party given in her honor by her colleagues and friends at the DA's office, Sotomayor was asked why she was leaving. Her questioner was Richard Girgente, who served as the deputy bureau chief for the office. Clearly, the DA's office at New York City could be a springboard to greater things such as a judgeship, political office, and even Morgenthau's job. It was clear by her deep commitment to the law, that Sotomayor had the makings of a first-rate prosecutor. So why was she leaving?

A TOUGH DECISION

Sotomayor's answer surprised Girgente. It was not the office, or certainly the lack of challenges. It was concern for Sotomayor's health. Given the fact that she was a diabetic, Sotomayor wanted to make sure she made the most of her time. The extreme stress that was part of working for the DA's office was hazardous enough for someone in good health. For someone with Sotomayor's condition, it could be debilitating, even life threatening.

Sotomayor's diabetes, while kept under control amid the chaos and bustle of the office, exhibited her highly developed discipline. Hugh M. Mo remembered how Sotomayor would come to his office to give herself a shot of insulin. If necessary, she would request a recess in court so that she could take her injections. Sotomayor even showed Mo how to give a shot in case she was unable to do so. Still, the stress and strain was such that Sotomayor had to weigh her love of the job with her future and her health. She decided that it was time to move on.[1]

Sotomayor also believed that she had an obligation to not only be the best lawyer she could be, but also to give back to the community that had given her so much. Girgente recalled, "She always viewed herself as a role model for Latino women in New York City, and she felt she had opportunities many others did not have and therefore had a higher responsibility to be a role model. There wasn't time to languish in one place." Sotomayor believed that because of all the opportunities she had been offered, much was expected of her in return. And that was alright with her. She believed she was now at a place where she could help others as she had been helped.[2]

MADISON AVENUE

By the time Sotomayor left the DA's office in 1984, private practice in the city of New York was exploding; in that year alone, the number of lawyers working in private firms across the country jumped to an astonishing 71 percent. This dramatic increase was the result of the growing demand for mergers and acquisition that had gripped the country and would mark much of the decade's legal and business dealings. During the period 1981 to 1989, the business world was rocked by a number of mergers that included the oil and gas industries, pharmaceuticals, banking, and airlines. There were also a number of foreign takeovers, many of them hostile, as a number of foreign companies bought up American businesses.[3]

To help with these new developments, law firms all over the country were on the lookout for eager, bright, and focused young lawyers. For someone with Sotomayor's background and credentials, it would not be hard to find a position with any number of the tony law firms in New York City. If anything, the problem would be in picking from the offers.

Sotomayor decided to go with the firm Pavia & Harcourt in April, 1984. The firm, which was located approximately two blocks from Central Park, housed its offices at 600 Madison Avenue. At that point, the firm had about 30 lawyers, which was considered small next to some of the large firms that employed hundreds of lawyers. The draw for Sotomayor was easy to see: not only would she gain experience in the practice of international law, but she would also continue to see the inside of a courtroom, something that the larger firms could not always promise to young lawyers because of the keen competition for cases.

Pavia & Harcourt was established in 1940, specifically to represent Italian fashion designers in the United States. It was also a boutique law firm, that is, a firm that specializes in a particular niche area of the law, unlike general practice law firms that typically cover a wide range of specialties. Boutique firms tend to be small, with often less than 100 attorneys. Pavia & Harcourt's niche was in business law. The firm concentrated on commercial and corporate law, banking, media and entertainment, real estate, litigation and arbitration, intellectual property, estate planning and administration, and immigration services. In addition to the firm's office in New York, Pavia & Harcourt also had offices in Milan, Italy, and Paris. Many of the firm's attorneys were fluent in a number of languages including French, Italian, and Spanish. The firm dealt with individuals, companies, government organizations, and various agencies. Most of the firm's clients, however, were European companies seeking to enter U.S. markets. Stephen Skulnik, a former member of the firm, described the firm's purpose: "If somebody's got a product or a service they want to distribute elsewhere, that's the firm's bread and butter."[4]

The firm was extremely interested in Sotomayor and pursued her to come and join them. Richard Mattiaccio, who had recently joined the firm remembers that, "We worked hard to recruit her . . . She had other options." In return Sotomayor was intrigued with the possibility of coming to work for Pavia & Harcourt. Mattiaccio described the firm at that time as "a hands-on practice and a dynamic atmosphere. . . . There was a lot of European investment in the U.S. at the time. She wanted to try cases and argue in court, rather than be a mid-level person on a large legal team [at a large law firm]." And so it was in April 1984 that Sotomayor found herself working for the firm.[5]

TO WORK

The firm began training their new hire in the field of civil litigation. Sotomayor showed herself to be a quick study. With her background as an assistant DA and knowledge of Spanish, Sotomayor was soon working on a number of challenging cases. George M. Pavia, the managing partner of the firm, described Sotomayor as "an excellent lawyer, a careful preparer of cases." In addition, Pavia was impressed with Sotomayor's confidence in the courtroom, particularly for the kind of cases that the firm dealt with. In a later interview, Pavia stated "Litigation is a particular side of the law that requires a great number of assets. They have to be quick on their feet, they have to be good citizens."[6]

To bring Sotomayor up to speed, she would attend weekly meetings with everyone in the firm. Because Pavia & Harcourt was such a small firm, it was easy to keep track of what everyone was doing. Richard Mattiaccio described the process: "We would get together and talk about our cases and share our ideas for how to handle them on a regular basis. The youngest associate would be there and get the benefit of being in that discussion; you learn what the considerations are." These meetings also offered everyone the chance to weigh the suggestions or other perspectives of their cases.[7]

For Mattiaccio, Sotomayor's arrival was timely. "I remember being so relieved when I heard she was coming, because we were very busy at the time," he recalled. In 1984, the firm was finding plenty of work with new clients hoping to begin selling their products in the American marketplace. But with each new client, came new problems, disputes, litigation, and more headaches for the lawyers.[8]

Working for Pavia & Harcourt provided Sotomayor with a wide range of challenges in the types of cases she would take on. At one point she might be settling a shipping dispute or defending a manufacturer from its American franchise. She also handled real estate cases, customs issues, product liability cases as well as trademark litigation. She also handled arbitration hearings, many on behalf of foreign buyers of American grains. Mattiaccio explained that the arbitration cases were "a very narrow, specialized area, but it's a lot like maritime practice because very often you're dealing with a shipload of grain. . . . there are usually large stakes involved."[9]

Sotomayor's clients represented some of the most recognizable makers of luxury and high-end products in the world: the luxury car maker Ferrari, Pirelli Tire, and the fashion house of Fendi. She also represented clients from banking industries.

Still, Sotomayor's days at the firm did not differ much from her DA days in terms of intensity. She continued to work long hours and at times would be so intent on her work, that she would not hear her colleagues calling to her or even fire alarms. "I'd say, 'Hello, Sonia,' and she'd never hear me," recalled Steven Skulnik, who worked with Sotomayor at Pavia & Harcourt, "She never had that fake intensity a lot of lawyers put on. Hers was completely genuine." In an interview in 1986, Sotomayor described what life as a lawyer in a top firm was really like: "The vast majority of lawyering is drudgery work—it's sitting in a library, it's banging out a brief, it's talking to clients for endless hours. . . . You miss a certain amount of maturity in those years, an emotional maturity."[10]

COUNTERFEITING CASES

During her second year of working for Pavia & Harcourt, Sotomayor became more involved with the legal issues surrounding the counterfeiting of luxury goods. During the 1980s, the counterfeiting of luxury items such as watches, handbags, toys, and sports team merchandise was a big business. During the 1970s and the 1980s though, counterfeiting was considered a small-time criminal enterprise, where unlicensed vendors would peddle cheap knockoffs on the street corners or out of car trunks. It was clear that the item was often of poor quality that came at a cheap price. At that point, many companies manufacturing luxury items were not too concerned about the counterfeiting of their goods.[11]

That idea began to change when a number of fashion houses began democratizing their goods, offering more moderately priced lines of clothing, handbags, or other items that bore the logo of the company but still made the item available at a lower price for middle-income buyers. However, this attempt to reach a greater number of people also had the consequences of even more counterfeit goods flooding the market. It was also becoming a growing concern for many European companies. By the early 1980s, an estimated $5 billion was finding its way into the pockets of counterfeiters. In New York City alone, it was estimated that approximately $350 million was lost in tax revenue from the sale of illegal products.[12]

In 1985, Sotomayor, working with one of the partners at Pavia & Harcourt, the late Frances Bernstein, created Fendi's national anticounterfeiting program. At this time, the sale of counterfeit goods was nothing more than a misdemeanor, which was rarely enforced. What Sotomayor and Bernstein hoped to do was to break new ground in counterfeiting prosecution, by first, going after counterfeiting and piracy rings and prosecuting them, and second, to raise public awareness of the crime and its effects on industries and the public.[13]

GOING TO THE STREETS

From 1985 to 1992, Sotomayor devoted most of her energies to the Fendi's anticounterfeiting program. (By 1988, Sotomayor was the head of the program.) Her duties were varied but included applying for injunctions every two or so months to seize counterfeit goods from street vendors and retailers suspected of selling counterfeit goods. She was a good fit for the job. Alessandro Saracino, in a 2009 interview, stated, "With her criminal law background, she was able to use her experience prosecuting violent crimes, organizing complex cases and working with the police. . . . [You have to remember that the general concept at that time was that knockoffs of designer goods were somewhat normal. It was a bit daring to go after counterfeiters.] Judges were very cautious about ordering seizures, and Sotomayor was able to present very compelling cases on behalf of the trademark owners."[14]

But doing battle in the courtroom was not all that Sotomayor did while working on the counterfeiting cases. More often than not, one might find her working on the streets to catch counterfeiters and their knockoffs. These outings provided some of the more colorful aspects of Sotomayor's time at Pavia & Harcourt. In a 1997 speech to the International Anticounterfeiting Coalition Meeting in Washington, D.C., Sotomayor stated: "My investigative experience with the Manhattan D.A.'s office came in handy when I found myself doing anticounterfeiting work on behalf of Fendi and other trademark owners." She then went on to describe what may have been a typical day at the office: "I particularly enjoyed the many lovely afternoons in Chinatown spent, wearing a bulletproof vest, with Heather McDonald the 'Dragon Lady,' as she was affectionately called by the local vendors, seizing counterfeit goods from the nooks and crannies that many of us never imagined existed within the maze of buildings that is Chinatown."[15]

The Dragon Lady, Heather McDonald, was a top-notch lawyer who specialized in intellectual property enforcement and anticounterfeiting litigation with another firm. The two met in 1987 at a conference of the International Anticounterfeiting Coalition. As McDonald later recalled, "We instantly hit it off, talking about our clients and the similar problems we were having. . . . We joined forces on the enforcement front because it was more cost effective and made a bigger impact." McDonald would go on to become a legend in Chinatown, where her photo was taped to walls and counters of the many shops found on Canal Street. One store owner even went so far as to have a red, slashed out circle—the international sign for "no"—imposed over McDonald's picture as if to say: "Watch Out for this Woman—She Will Take Your Stuff!"[16]

Usually the team followed a pretty straight scenario in tracking down counterfeiters. Relying on tips from U.S. Customs agents, the firms would learn about suspicious cargo coming into the country and its location: often a warehouse, basement, or store. Once information had been received about locations where counterfeit goods could be found, the firms would acquire warrants and then would send in investigators, usually posing as tourists, to purchase the knock-off goods, which were then turned over to the client to inspect. The law firms generally pooled their resources and used the same investigators who would buy a number of different types of products representing any number of companies such as Fendi, Chanel, Gucci, Rolex, or Cartier. Often when confronted, the merchants in question would react angrily to the seizure of their goods. This did not stop Sotomayor, who often accompanied police on their busts. As George Pavi recalled, "On several occasions she went in wearing a Kevlar vest and seized the goods. . . . We won victory after victory" when cases finally went to court.[17]

Much as she waded into drug dens and back alleys as an assistant DA, Sotomayor had no qualms about being as hands on as she could get in her newest role. On any given day, she might be walking through dirty, dank basement areas, looking at fake Rolex watches or Fendi handbags. On one occasion, while trying to bust a group of counterfeiters selling merchandise at Shea Stadium, Sotomayor hopped on the back of a motorcycle to give chase. As she later told an audience, "I have never gotten back on a motorcycle after that day, when I belatedly realized that cars were much bigger than motorcycles, and that I had lost reason in the heat of pursuit by ever getting on the motorcycle as a passenger at all."[18]

Heather McDonald remembers how the two women "spent a lot of time together in the back of police vans with the windows blacked out. . . . Frankly, it was a little bit like the Wild West in those days. Counterfeiting had just become illegal with the passage of a federal law in 1984 [which allowed civil seizures of counterfeit goods], and this was the early days of enforcement. There was the possibility of violence and we had bodyguards that stuck to us like glue. But as in her entire career, Sonia was a worker: she got right into those dirty basements you can imagine what they looked like and took inventory of the counterfeit merchandise."[19]

Steven Skulnik occasionally worked with Sotomayor and remembered how in one instance, he and Sotomayor, accompanied by the police descended on a suspected counterfeiting operation in a Harlem storefront. "I was crouched in the van, waiting for things to clear up, and Sonia goes running out with the investigators," Skulnik said in a 2009 interview. "She got a thrill out of the cops and robbers stuff. It's not something you expect to see from a corporate attorney."[20]

THE FENDI CRUSH

One of Sotomayor's clients suffering from counterfeiting was Fendi, a well-known Italian design company that included luxury leather goods such as handbags and shoes. The fashion house was created in 1925 by a young couple, Edoardo and Adele Fendi, as a handbag and fur shop, located in the Via del Plebiscito, Rome. In time, the shop began to attract attention for its stylish products and quality. For many of the Roman bourgeoisie, shopping trips soon included a stop to "Fendi at the Plebiscito." By the 1930s and 1940s, the fur workshop expanded and the Fendi name became more widely known outside of Rome.[21]

By 1946, the Fendi's five daughters began working in the family business. The daughters developed new products for the fashion house's leather and fur sections. The family business was also aided with the hiring of an up-and-coming fashion designer from Paris by the name Karl Lagerfeld. Under Lagerfeld's direction, the fur designs underwent a dramatic retooling with changes in materials, design, and production. It was also during this period that the Fendi logo, consisting of the "double F" design was first rolled out.[22]

Beginning in the 1960s and 1970s, Fendi added a prêt-a-porter collection, or ready-to-wear collection of furs. The design house's signature bag was also redesigned offering customers bags that were more soft and unstructured as opposed to popular bags with a more rigid form. The leather was also printed, woven, dyed, and tanned in order to make it softer to the touch and more attractive to the eye. By 1977, the Fendi family turned its energies to clothing and began designing a haute couture line that included ties, gloves, jeans, home furnishings, sunglasses, and even perfume.

By the 1980s and early 1990s, the Fendi logo was one of the most popular targets for counterfeiters. During this period, a typical Fendi handbag might normally retail for $350, while a counterfeit could be purchased for anywhere from $25 to $75. The company, now in the hands of the five daughters retained the services of Pavia & Harcourt to deal with the problem. Handling the company's claims was Sonia Sotomayor.

By 1987, Fendi had uncovered widespread counterfeit activity not only in New York City's Chinatown but also in a number of retail stores, including the national chain store Burlington Coat Factory. Fendi claimed that the retail chain was knowingly purchasing Fendi knock-offs that included handbags, perfumes, and other items. Sotomayor decided to take the retailer to court and acted as the sole attorney during the trial. In the end, the case was settled in Fendi's favor with Burlington having to pay financial compensation as well as being served with a court injunction prohibiting the retailer from buying or selling any Fendi merchandise, unless they had written permission from the company.[23]

In the meantime, Sotomayor was faced with another problem: how to get rid of all the counterfeit Fendi merchandise that had been accumulated during the numerous raids over the last few years. Sotomayor came up with a novel way of not only taking care of the problem but also calling attention to legal victories her client had won for pursuing counterfeiters. And so it was on the morning of November 12, 1986, Carla Fendi, who had flown in to take part in the publicity event, presided over the unusual spectacle taking place outside New York City's landmark restaurant Tavern on the Green. As Fendi, Sotomayor, and an assorted group of spectators watched, thousands of fake Fendi bags, wallets, shoes, and other accessories first had paint poured over them and then were fed into garbage trucks where they were then crushed. The original plan had been to have a huge bonfire to burn the fake goods, but the New York City Fire Department stopped that idea cold. Instead, Sotomayor came up with the idea that would be known as the Fendi Crush.[24]

As Sotomayor looked on at the spectacle, she was interviewed by a *New York Times* reporter. She told her interviewer that going after counterfeiters was a lot like chasing drug dealers:

> We attempt to go after suppliers and secure information that leads back to the manufacturers. We go after U.S. retailers to the degree that we send cease-and-desist orders and request that they voluntarily cooperate and turn over the counterfeits.
>
> We have yet to meet a retail seller who admits "I knew." It is our position that if they had used a standard of diligence and compared them to a genuine Fendi, they would have known.[25]

The Fendi Crush, not only garnered publicity for the Fendi company but also for Sotomayor and her firm. As George Pavia later described, "In the presence of the press . . . we threw masses and masses of handbags, shoes, and other items into these garbage trucks. It was the pinnacle of our achievement, and Sonia was the principal doer."[26]

TOUGHENING THE LAWS

Sotomayor enjoyed tracking down counterfeiters and taking them to court, but she knew that if her work was to have any long-lasting effect, there should be tougher laws in place. In 1990, working with Heather Mc Donald, Sotomayor played a key role in drafting anticounterfeiting legislation that became part of the New York state penal code. McDonald recalling their work stated that "It was the first law in New York state that made the sale of counterfeit merchandise illegal. . . . We spent a lot of time working on that together, and we were the principal drafters of the original legislation. We worked with industry lobbyists and lawmakers to make it law."[27]

Yet, the process was also a frustrating one for the lawyers. McDonald described their time working with the New York state legislature as an interesting but frustrating experience because of the manner in which laws are drafted, voted on, and put into place. Overall, the experience, McDonald told a reporter, was eye opening: "You go there thinking very idealistically, 'You've got a problem and we've got a solution, but there was so much deal making and back door negotiating to try to get something done.'" When the bill finally passed in 1991, Sotomayor and McDonald were ecstatic. "I remember," McDonald said, "having a conversation with her in which we said, 'Now we have to get somebody arrested under this law.'"[28]

The law that eventually passed—New York State Penal Code Statutes 165.70, 165.71, 165.72, and 165.73—defines three levels of trademark counterfeiting. This includes a misdemeanor charge that involved the manufacturing or selling of a counterfeit item with a value below $1,000. The next level involves counterfeiting activity of goods valued more than $1,000 and is considered a Class E felony; the last level of counterfeiting crimes being defined as trafficking in counterfeit goods worth over $100,000, making it a Class C felony.

Sotomayor was hopeful that with New York breaking new ground in counterfeiting and illegal trademark crimes, other states would soon follow with similar laws. In an interview with the *San Francisco Chronicle* in 1992, she stated, "In the next five or ten years, trademark owners will become more concentrated on changing state laws, changing penalties. They will rely more on local police to make arrests. A real threat of jail does have an impact." But Sotomayor also was enough of a realist to recognize that even with stiffer penalties in place and more aggressive policing, counterfeiters would always be around, as long as there was a way to make an easy buck.[29]

OFF HOURS

Even though her long days at Pavia & Harcourt kept her extremely busy, Sotomayor did find time to socialize with her colleagues, sometimes grabbing lunch at a nearby corner restaurant, McCann's, where she indulged in hamburgers and onion rings. She maintained her modest apartment in Carroll Gardens in Brooklyn where she frequented many of the Italian restaurants in the neighborhood. Sotomayor also took time to travel: among her destinations was Israel in 1986, where she accompanied a group of Hispanic leaders as part of an exchange educational program. Richard Mattiaccio recalled that Sotomayor developed a real love of traveling and given her salary, she made the most of any opportunity to travel to new places. Her increased income also allowed her to be generous toward family and friends, often loaning them money, treating them to meals or an outing, or buying them gifts.[30]

In addition, Sotomayor also believed strongly in giving back to her community. To that end, she made an on-going commitment to doing pro bono work, or working for free to various boards, which included the Puerto Rican Legal Defense and Education Fund, now known as LatinoJustice PRLDEF. She came to the organization in 1980, just as she was getting out of law school. She was chosen to take the place of José Cabranes, her mentor at Yale, on the board. Cesar Perales, who founded the PRLDEF recalled that "She was very young at the time . . . José Cabranes recommended her to the board as someone who would bring young blood and new ideas. He had sensed from her interests that she would like serving on our board." Sotomayor also served in a number of leadership positions in the organization such as first vice president and chair of the Litigation and Education Committees.[31]

MOVING UP

In addition to her pro bono activities, Sotomayor was also tending to her other ambitions. Many years earlier, in a conversation with her boss, Robert M. Morgenthau, Sotomayor stated that corporate law held little attraction for her. Again confronted with the specter of her diabetes, Sotomayor felt a sense of urgency about her life. "It made her think, 'I'm not going to be around forever, I have to keep moving,'"

Morgenthau said. "I remember talking with her about how much time each day, about an hour, she spent giving herself shots of insulin."[32]

One of Sotomayor's goals was to serve on a public board for the city. Not only would the experience give her greater exposure to the city and its leaders, it would also provide her with the necessary experience to continue moving up the ladder for public service positions. Aiding her in this were not people in the traditional higher circles of power such as political party leaders or other politicians. Instead, her champion was her former boss, Morgenthau, who tapped into his extensive network to help land Sotomayor a seat on the Campaign Finance Board. The fact that Sotomayor was an extremely accomplished lawyer with formidable credentials, at a time when diversity in the more traditional white male spheres of influence was sought, also helped.[33]

FIRST STEPS

In 1987, while at Pavia & Harcourt, Sotomayor talked with one of the partners in the firm, David Botwinik, who, along with a close friend mentioned Sotomayor's interest in public service to then-governor Mario Cuomo. In the meantime, Sotomayor thought about applying for the counsel's job at the state's Urban Development Corporation. She even went so far as to talk with the woman who was leaving the job, Susan Heilbron, who later stated in an interview that her talk with Sotomayor, "blew my socks off." Heilbron then told Sotomayor that, "With all due respect, the kind of public service you ought to be doing is bigger than this."[34]

Instead, the governor's appointments secretary, Ellen E. Conovitz, recommended that Sotomayor be appointed as a board member of Sonyma, the state mortgage agency, which provided below-market-rate mortgages for the needy. The board was badly in need of direction as well as fresh blood and it helped that Sotomayor could also bring diversity to the board. By all accounts, Sotomayor took her job as seriously as she took her cases, pushing board members to redirect more monies to lower-income homeowners.[35]

During her time at the agency, which lasted from 1987 to 1991, Sotomayor proved herself to be a somewhat controversial member. During that time Sonyma was responsible for the insuring of hundreds of millions of dollars in mortgages, and was also responsible for the construction of thousands of apartments for moderate-income New York residents. But in spite of the board's aims, Sotomayor often expressed doubt and uneasiness with the thrust of the programs. For one thing, she objected to the rehabilitation of projects in low-income areas, in which lower-income families might be displaced. Even though she often voted for many of the projects that came across the board's table, she still voiced concerns over who the projects ultimately benefitted. Her tough and skeptical questioning made sure that the board kept its focus on the poor. Royce Mulholland, who worked with the Division of Housing and Community Renewal and who also served on the board, remembered that Sotomayor "wanted lower-income people served, and that's a good goal. . . . But we also explained that the insurance program was intended to serve moderate- and middle-income apartments—and we only provided the insurance, which means we had very little leverage."[36]

There were also problems among the board members. Even though the state encouraged diversity, it was not always welcomed. "It was like a boys' club when we came there," recalled Hazel Dukes, an African American who joined the board around the same time as Sotomayor. But as Dukes later stated, "We knew how to be pushy. We were like bees in their bonnet." One former board member, Fioravante G. Perrotta, was quite vocal in his dislike of Sotomayor. Perrotta, who admitted that Sotomayor was quite conscientious and knowledgeable, was also an "extreme partisan" when it came to issues of class and ethnicity. "She made it very clear that she was very liberal and a Democrat," said Perrotta in a 2009 interview, "and that really should have been a nonpolitical organization."[37]

CAMPAIGN FINANCE BOARD

A year later, in 1988, Sotomayor was appointed to the Campaign Finance Board with the help of her mentor, Robert Morgenthau. What made Sotomayor's appointment all the more unusual was the fact that she did not conform to the typical New York City political party dynamic. Although Sotomayor often took a liberal stance on many matters, it did not automatically guide her into the traditional liberal fold of the Democratic Party. In a city where Democrats outnumber Repub-

licans, five to one, Sotomayor was a registered independent voter, a fact
that no doubt increased her desirability to the city's politicians.

The Campaign Board arose out of a needed response to the city's
corruption scandals, with the board serving as a kind of policing force
that oversaw campaign spending and doled out matching funds. During that period, then-Mayor Edward Koch was given two appointments
for the board, of which one could be a Democrat and the other, an
independent or a Republican. Peter L. Zimroth, who served as Mayor
Koch's counsel, wanted to see a board member with a prosecutorial
background. He then called Morgenthau, who in turn, recommended
Sotomayor. In fact, Sotomayor would be the only person interviewed
by Zimroth, who later stated, "I remember when I finished the interview
thinking that we had found a gem, that this was a straight shooter, a
very serious lawyer who seemed absolutely independent."[38]

Over the next four years, Sotomayor and the board oversaw and
ruled on matters pertaining to city campaigns, which included the
mayoral races of David Dinkins and Rudolph Giuliani. To the other
board members, Sotomayor was a dogged and sometimes demanding
member. Nicole A. Gordon, who served as executive director of the
board remembered that Sotomayor "had no patience for candidates
who tried the 'dog ate my homework' defense." Another board member, the Rev. Joseph A. O'Hare called her "tenacious" stating, "We
would be in a tense interview with a candidate and she would be shoot-
ing herself with insulin in the back of the hand."[39]

Somehow between her demanding duties at Pavia & Harcourt and
her commitments to public service, Sotomayor also found time to work
on other panels and boards such as the Maternity Center that sought
to improve maternity care through research and educational activities.
She also served as a member of the Selection Committee for the Stan-
ley D. Heckman Educational Fund that provided monies for college
scholarships for high-school students. She also worked on Governor
Cuomo's Advisory Panel for Inter-Group Relations that provides solu-
tions for group-conflict resolution.

Sotomayor still found time for fun. She attended the ballet, the
opera, and rock concerts. She cheered on her beloved Yankees and
took in an occasional Broadway show. She lived the life of a true New
Yorker. But even with all the activity swirling around her, Sotomayor

knew there was more to accomplish. Whether taking down counterfeiters in Chinatown, fighting for housing for the poor, or yelling at the Yankees to win another one, she still kept her eye on the next rung of the ladder.[40]

NOTES

1. Antonia Felix, *Sonia Sotomayor: The True American Dream*, New York: Berkeley Publishing Group, 2010, p. 96.

2. Ibid.

3. Ibid.; EconomyWatch, "History of Mergers and Acquisitions," http://www.economywatch.com/mergers-acquisitions/history.html.

4. Pavia & Harcourt, "Our Profile," http://www.pavialaw.com/profile.cfm; Karen Sloan, "Sotomayor's Civil Practice was with a Small, but Specialized Firm," *National Law Journal*, May 28, 2009, http://www.law.com/jsp/nlj/PubArticleNLJ.jsp?id=1202431049336.

5. Sloan, "Sotomayor's Civil Practice was with a Small, but Specialized Firm."

6. John D. McKinnon, "Sotomayor: Fighting for . . . Fendi?," *Wall Street Journal*, May 26, 2009, http://blogs.wsj.com/washwire/2009/05/26/sotomayor-fighting-forfendi/.

7. Felix, *Sonia Sotomayor*, p. 118.

8. Ibid., p. 116.

9. Ibid., p. 118.

10. Michael Powell, "To Get to Sotomayor's Core, Go to New York," *New York Times*, July 9, 2009, http://www.nytimes.com/2009/07/10/nyregion/10sonia.html?pagewanted=all.

11. Dana Thomas, "The Cost of Counterfeiting," *Lo$t*, December 2008-January 2009, http://www.lostmag.com/issue29/counterfeiting.php.

12. Ibid.; Felix, *Sonia Sotomayor*, p. 119.

13. Felix, *Sonia Sotomayor*, p. 119.

14. David Lipke, "Judge Sotomayor's Fashionable Past (Sonia Sotomayor)" *Women's Wear Daily*, July 1, 2009, http://www.accessmylibrary.com/article-1G1–203645860/judge-sotomayor-fashionable-past.html.

15. "Quotes," Baker Hostetler, July 13, 2010, http://www.bakerlaw.com/articles/sonia-sotomayor-the-true-american-dream-07–13–2010/; Lipke, "Judge Sotomayor's Fashionable Past (Sonia Sotomayor)"

16. "Quotes," Baker Hostetler.

17. McKinnon, "Sotomayor: Fighting for . . . Fendi?"

18. Lipke, "Judge Sotomayor's Fashionable Past (Sonia Sotomayor)"

19. Ibid.

20. Sloan, "Sotomayor's Civil Practice was with a Small, but Specialized Firm."

21. "The History of Fendi," http://www.fendi.com/#/en/forever fendi/historyoffendi.

22. Ibid.

23. Felix, *Sonia Sotomayor*, pp. 130–31.

24. McKinnon, "Sotomayor: Fighting for . . . Fendi?"

25. Michael Gross, "Fashion Notes," *New York Times*, November 11, 1986, A16.

26. Martha Neil, "Fendi Crush was Highlight of Sotomayor's IP Practice," *ABA Journal*, May 26, 2009, http://www.abajournal.com/news/article/fendi_crush_was_highlight_of_sotomayors_ip_practice.

27. "Quotes," Baker Hostetler.

28. Ibid.

29. Trish Donnally, "Fashion's Assault on Counterfeiters; Companies Fight to Stop Others Cashing in on Their Good Name," *San Francisco Chronicle*, May 20, 1992, p. D3.

30. Felix, *Sonia Sotomayor*, pp. 139–40.

31. Ibid., pp. 140–41.

32. Michael Powell and Serge Kovaleski, "Sotomayor Rose on Merit Alone, Her Allies Say," *New York Times*, June 4, 2009, http://www.nytimes.com/2009/06/05/us/politics/05judge.html.

33. Ibid.

34. Ibid.

35. Ibid.

36. Charlie Savage and Michael Powell, "Sotomayor Put Focus on the Poor," *New York Times*, June 18, 2009, http://www.tmg-housing.com/PDF/Sotomayor.pdf.

37. Ibid.

38. Powell and Kovaleski, "Sotomayor Rose on Merit Alone, Her Allies Say."

39. Ibid.

40. Felix, *Sonia Sotomayor*, p. 144.

Chapter 7

"YOU'RE OUT!"

On February, 15, 1991, a small article ran in the *New York Times* titled, "Now, No Hispanic Candidates For Federal Bench in New York." The article detailed the decision of Judge John Carro, the sole Hispanic candidate for the federal district court in Manhattan, to withdraw his name from consideration for a position on the bench of the Southern District Court, a division of the Federal Justice system. Carro, then serving as a justice for the appellate division of the New York State Supreme Court, had waited for three years for an answer from the White House for his possible appointment to the post. By all accounts, Carro was considered to be an eminent jurist and, according to the America Bar Association, was rated "highly qualified" as a judge.[1]

In his letter to United States Senator Daniel Patrick Moynihan, who represented the state of New York, Carro stated what many others had suspected privately for the last three years. Carro was withdrawing his name for consideration because he could "only assume" that then-President George H. W. Bush's failure to consider his nomination was "because he disagrees with the views I have expressed in the opinions I have written in over 20 years on the bench." It was a resounding criticism not only of the president but also of the White House and its politics, particularly in the area of diversity. One anonymous member of Congress, privy to the nomination process summed up the situation succinctly with the statement, "It's clear the White House simply didn't want him."[2]

A GLARING ABSENCE

Technically, the appointment of federal judges is done by the President of the United States who often makes his choice by relying on recommendations of the senate, who must also consent to the appointment. This scenario lends itself to a situation in which the president seeks out the advice of the more learned men of both political parties. But the reality is much different and is more in keeping with the practice of political patronage and rewards. Candidates for the federal bench in any state are often offered to the White House by the senior senator from the president's party, in Bush's case, the Republicans. In the case of New York, the senior senator was Alfonse M. D'Amato.

But where New York was concerned, there was also a long-standing arrangement put in place that allowed both parties to select nominees to the federal bench. Many years earlier, Moynihan and the late Republican Senator Jacob Javits decided on this bipartisan approach to selecting judicial candidates. The two men agreed that when the state's two senators belonged to different parties, each senator would share the recommendations with the other. It was also decided that the senator of the same party as the president, selected three out of the four federal judge appointees; the senator from the other party would have one recommendation. By the time Bush entered the White House, Republican Senator Alfonse D'Amato could recommend three candidates for the federal bench and Senator Moynihan one candidate. It was under this arrangement that Moynihan recommended Carro in 1988.[3]

The refusal to appoint Carro was more than a political slap in the face; it also suggested that the White House was not interested in moving very quickly to take care of what was a very real and pressing need for the five federal benches in New York that by 1991, had four vacancies, one of which had been empty for almost three years. Not only that, the seeming dismissal of any Hispanic candidate in a state came at a time when the population of the United States was changing dramatically.

By 1991, the Hispanic population had increased in the United States by 53 percent, making the population jump more than five times that of the total United States population. By 1991, approximately 25 million or almost 10 percent of the people living in the United States were Hispanic. New York, along with Texas, California, and Florida had seen a dramatic increase in the number of Hispanics living and working in the state. According to the 1990 census, of the 17,990,445 residents living in New York, approximately 2,214,026 were Hispanics, making up roughly 12 percent of the total population. In New York City, over 1.8 million Hispanics were among the population while in Bronx County, where Sonia Sotomayor grew up, more than 523,000 Hispanics resided, accounting for 43.5 percent of the total Hispanic population in the state.[4]

The scarcity of Hispanic judges on the federal bench during the Bush administration was particularly galling to Hispanics across the United States. For the Bush administration, the problem was also a political one; census projections suggested that Hispanics were poised to become the largest identifiable minority in the country by the 21st century. This fact was not lost on Bush, who had worked hard to draw Hispanic support during his 1988 campaign.[5]

Given the sizable Hispanic population in the state, the criticism over the lack of Hispanic judges was particularly sharp. The absence of Hispanic judges in New York was a stark contrast to what was happening in other areas of the nation where there were sizable Hispanic populations. For instance, two Hispanic judges were appointed to the federal district courts in Florida, while California had three Hispanic justices; there was also one Hispanic judge on the federal bench in Arizona.[6]

When the news of Carro's withdrawal was made public, neither the White House nor Senator Moynihan had any comment. However, the Hispanic community in New York City had plenty to talk about. For years, the notable absence of any Hispanic federal judges had become a sticking point among the Hispanic community. Frank Torres, a justice of the New York Supreme Court in Manhattan, writing in the January issue of the *New York State Bar Journal* reflected that Hispanic judges are underrepresented in general on the federal bench, "but conspicuously so in New York, which is a state with one of the largest Hispanic populations in the nation." Torres went on to state that despite the growing Hispanic population in New York state, which included approximately 2,000 Hispanic lawyers, there was still no Hispanic presence on the federal bench. "This absence," Torres remarked, "is viewed by many Hispanics as a vestige of American unequal opportunity and racial discrimination."[7]

PLAYING POLITICS

Many years later, when asked who was responsible for Sotomayor's career as a federal court judge. Judah Gribetz, who had worked for Senator Moynihan, joked, "I'm the fellow that was the culprit." In reality, the process of nominating Sotomayor for one of the vacant slots on the New York state federal bench was almost as straightforward as Gribetz's comment. It also provides a revealing look at the realities of New York politics, and how Sotomayor's nomination proved to be all the more remarkable.[8]

Around the same time that the Democrats began a new search for nominee to the federal bench, David Botwinik and David Glasser, two lawyers at the law firm Pavia & Harcourt, called their friend Judah Gribetz. Gribetz was the chairman of the judiciary screening committee of Senator Moynihan. The purpose of Botwinik and Glasser's call was to recommend their partner, Sonia Sotomayor, for a position on the federal bench as a judge. Gribetz later recalled that Botwinik and Glasser told him that "She was somebody. . . . 'You know how everybody's talking about how the country is evolving? Here's a gal that came out of the South Bronx and went to Princeton and Yale, was in Bob Morgenthau's office and is at Pavia & Harcourt, a nice law firm. She has a future.'" When Gribetz decided to go ahead and put Sotomayor's name in front of the senator, he was asked, "Where did you find her, Judah?" Gribetz replied, "She came out of nowhere."[9]

Gribetz's comment is a revealing one, for up until that point, Sotomayor was a blip on the New York political screen. Even with her work with the LatinoJustice PRLDEF, the State Mortgage Board, and other agencies, Sotomayor was not being championed by the traditional power brokers of New York politics such as mayors, congressional representatives, or senators. When questioned about her years later, local party bosses could honestly say they remembered nothing about her. With the possible exception of Robert Morgenthau who contacted people on her behalf, no one can really claim to having mentored Sotomayor through the political process, which is a remarkable occurrence and a bit of an aberration in New York City and state politics.[10]

Still, the timing was right for someone like Sotomayor. At the age of 38, she had already distinguished herself as tough prosecutor, as well as a savvy litigator. She plunged headfirst into her work and seemed capable of applying her razor sharp legal instincts as well as showing a genuine compassion for the poor and overlooked. She was also a Latina woman at a time when the issue of diversity was something that white males in power could not afford to dismiss so easily. Gribetz recalled, "If you live in the end of the 20th century, there was nothing incompatible between diversity and excellence. . . . Obviously we were looking for people who were representative, and with the right credentials. . . . [Sotomayor] fit the bill." Gribetz also went on to state, "Let's talk about how judges are made. . . . Sonia had no political connections and did not come through the political process, but these were social friends of mine. I trusted them."[11]

MEETING THE SENATOR

Moynihan remembers that the first time he heard of Sotomayor as a potential nominee, his judicial selection staff told him, "Have we got a judge for you!" Moynihan was intrigued enough to look over Sotomayor's qualifications and to agree to set up an interview with the prospective nominee. Nick Allard, who many years before had worked with Sotomayor in the Princeton University cafeteria, and who was now heavily involved in the state's Democratic party recalled how he had received a phone call from Chester Straub, then-head of Moynihan's judicial selection committee about Sotomayor. In a 2009 interview, Allard stated that while in a meeting with Moynihan, he "vividly remember[ed] saying, 'Sonia Sotomayor is terrific, and she should be the head of any list.' And Moynihan, in his stammering, sarcastic staccato, looked at me and said, 'Some news flash. Like telling me DiMaggio can hit.'"[12]

In the meantime, Sotomayor was being vetted by a selection committee of 12 to 20 people picked by Moynihan. Sotomayor was interviewed by lawyers, retired judges, and law professors. In addition, she
was required to fill out a very long questionnaire that asked a variety of
questions including her experience and qualifications in dealing with
federal and state courts. There were no questions about how she would
rule on a hypothetical legal issue. As Sotomayor recounted in a 2006
interview, "At that time, people were more sensitive. . . . The closest
it came was someone asked if I felt okay about the death penalty. My
response was no one should feel okay about the death penalty—that is
a serious matter—but if you are asking me can I follow the law that is
a different question."[13]

Joseph Gale, another former classmate of Sotomayor's from Princeton, was in Moynihan's chief tax council at the time of Sotomayor's
pending nomination. Gale recalled telling Moynihan, "Senator, anyone who won the Pyne Prize at Princeton is worth nominating to the
bench—it's a real mark of early achievement." Moynihan eventually
decided to interview Sotomayor in private before making any final decision. On the day of the interview Gale was also in the office. He
remembered Sotomayor's poise and composure when she met with
Moynihan. Gale later stated his amazement in part came from the fact
that "She was new to the political world and she just seemed to handle
that part of it well. I don't think she had much of a political background."[14]

At the end of the interview Moynihan was satisfied that Sotomayor
would be the best choice for the slot. Little did anyone realize that
Moynihan was at that moment, privately convinced that Sotomayor
had what it took to someday make her way to the Supreme Court as
the first Hispanic Justice on the bench. In March 1991, Moynihan announced Sotomayor as his nominee for the federal district court.[15]

The next step was contacting his colleague Senator Alfonse
D'Amato. In talking about Sotomayor's nomination, D'Amato stated
that he would meet with the prospective candidate to see how well
she did with him and his committee. "When she came to meet with
me and I checked with my committee, they agreed that she was outstanding," he later said. D'Amato then presented Sotomayor's nomination to the Bush administration. Initially, the Justice Department

opposed Moynihan and D'Amato's recommendation, but Mr. D'Amato claims that he intervened on Sotomayor's behalf. "I had a pretty good relationship with them [the administration]," D'Amato recalled, "and I said, 'We have this agreement and we were going to honor it.' They didn't like [it] but they took it." D'Amato later stated that part of the problem was that rumors had begun circulating about Sotomayor as a future prospect for Supreme Court; as a result, Republican opposition to Sotomayor occupying any seat on the bench had already been set in motion.[16]

Next Sotomayor was reviewed by the Standing Committee on Federal Judiciary of the American Bar Association who reviewed her legal career. The committee then issued a report with their findings, which supported Moynihan and D'Amato's recommendation that Sotomayor was a qualified candidate for the federal bench. She also received a number of endorsements from various people who had worked with her and who stressed her deep-seated commitment to justice, her desire to better her community, and her willingness to be of service. More than a few also pointed out that by appointing Sotomayor to the federal bench, the Bush administration would be remembered by Hispanic voters.

But before Bush could announce that Sotomayor was his nominee for the position a setback occurred. In what was standard political procedure, Senator Moynihan had put a hold on two federal circuit court judges that the Bush administration hoped to confirm. The senator would lift the hold only if his district court nominees were approved. Once the president's administration and Moynihan came to an agreement, Sotomayor's nomination was green lighted. In November 1991, President Bush announced his nominee for a New York federal court judgeship: 38-year-old Sonia Sotomayor of New York City. Now all that was needed was a Senate confirmation; to that end, hearings on her nomination were scheduled for June 1992.[17]

Much later, Sotomayor stated that Moynihan was the "single most important person" behind her rise to the bench. She was keenly aware of the "enormous political capital" the senator had exerted on her behalf. For her own part, Sotomayor was feeling a "sense of disbelief" over her nomination. Being appointed to the third highest court in the country was a daunting proposition; many would want her to succeed, but perhaps even intimidating was the fact that there were as many who would also be very happy if she was to fail.[18]

CONFIRMED!

Seated before her on her first day of the U.S. Senate Judiciary Hearing in Washington, D.C., Sonia Sotomayor found herself being questioned by Committee Chairman, Senator Edward Kennedy. The chairman led Sotomayor through a number of questions including her pro bono legal activities as well as her experiences in the courtroom. At one point, Kennedy asked Sotomayor how she would "convince lawyers of the need to make real commitments to public service," to which she replied: "I, as an individual, believe that those of us who have opportunities in this life must give them back to those who have less. It is never easy to encourage others to do the same, but I do think it is important for public figures, for legal educators, for the bar to constantly and repeatedly encourage public service."[19]

Overall, the hearings went well, with Sotomayor maintaining a respectful and congenial rapport with the committee. Her vote was scheduled for August 11, 1992, after being delayed for several weeks for unknown political reasons, according to D'Amato. However, in the end Sotomayor was confirmed as a district-court judge with the unanimous consent of the Senate on August 11, 1992. As she later recounted, "The hearing was wonderful," she said later. "Because a Democratic senator had proposed me and a Republican President nominated me, my questions were pro forma." Her confirmation, in August 1992, made her the first Hispanic federal judge in the state of New York, and one of seven women among the 58 judges who served on the federal bench.[20] The very next day, on August 12, Sotomayor was back in New York City where she received her commission as a judge for the U.S. District Court for the Southern District of New York. Not more than two months later, on October 2, Sotomayor was sworn in at the Ceremonial Courtroom 506, located in the U.S. Courthouse at 40 Centre Street in New York City. Afterwards, Sotomayor was feted with a party held in her honor by Pavia & Harcourt. Her next move was to become familiar with a court docket that handled everything from drug cases to white-collar crime and securities litigation.[21]

500 PEARL STREET

During her first few weeks at her office at 500 Pearl Street, Sotomayor struggled with the mounds of material, including printed guidebooks, videos, and seminars that instructed baby judges on the inner workings of the district court. At times Sotomayor admitted she was terrified by the new role she was to undertake. In fact during her first year on the bench, she would go so far as to question as to whether she was ready to take on the duties of a federal judge. In Sotomayor's case, it was not insecurity that drove her so much to question her abilities, but whether she was ready to take up the tremendous responsibility of this new and very powerful position.[22]

Sotomayor, as junior judge, was housed on the sixth floor of the federal courthouse. She had a small office but no courtroom that was hers alone. Her office suite consisted of an entrance with desks for a secretary and a court deputy. One door to the left of the entrance room led to her chambers; the door to the right was reserved for an office used by two law clerks. Helping Sotomayor ease into her new position was her secretary from Pavia & Harcourt, Theresa Bartenope, who would remain with Sotomayor throughout her time on the bench. Bartenope was considered the soul and life of the office. Her warm personality would make Sotomayor's office an energetic and inviting place to work for everyone.

Sotomayor's first day at her new job gave her a sense of what lay before her. At 8:30 in the morning, as Sotomayor, Bartenope, and one of the new clerks were trying to unpack several of the 100 boxes of books brought to Sotomayor's office, the phone rang. Thinking that it was a friendly voice on the other end, wishing Sotomayor well on her first day, Bartenope was startled to hear a litigant telling her that his case had been assigned to Sotomayor and that the person wanted an immediate trial date. Bartenope put the caller on hold, turned to Sotomayor and asked, "Judge, what do I do?"[23]

As the morning went on, Sotomayor and one of her law clerks continued to unpack cartons of books and in general, try to get the office in order. They were startled at one point, by what sounded like a doorbell ringing. The clerk, Joseph Evall, a graduate of Harvard Law School, went to the door and upon opening it, saw some lawyers outside who had just filed an emergency request for a temporary restraining order

(TRO). The lawyers had also been told that Sotomayor was assigned as judge in their case. In the flurry of the next few minutes, the lawyers received their answers and Evall was able to turn back to his duties.[24]

Slowly Sotomayor and her staff settled into their new quarters. The judge learned how to use a computer, thanks to the help of her law clerks. Sotomayor took care with furnishing her office that included choosing colorful fabrics for the furniture. She also added a number of personal touches including photos of family and friends and a number of gavels that she had received as presents.[25]

If few people knew about Sotomayor before she took the bench, now more were learning about the new judge from the Bronx. In a profile piece done for the *New York Times* in 1992, not long after Sotomayor took the bench, the reporter noted:

> In person, with her round face and faint spray of summer freckles, Ms. Sotomayor looks younger than her 38 years and, wearing dangling earrings and a leather-and-gold bracelet, not every inch the judge. Neither does she have the studied charm nor dazzle factor of many judicial candidates who win accolades from lawyers and politicians. Hers is a cumulative impression. She is plain-spoken and direct, good-humored but not exactly humorous. She is also seemingly without affectation . . . "You know anybody who wants to buy my cheap apartment in Carroll Gardens?" she asks in a street-scraped New York accent, referring to the section of Brooklyn."[26]

Because of her new position, Sotomayor had to move to a residence in her current judicial district. She chose to move back to the Bronx. Her salary also dropped from $230,000 that she was earning at Pavia & Harcourt to a federal judge's salary of $129,000. The drop in pay did not faze her. In an interview, Sotomayor stated, "I've never wanted to get adjusted to my income because I knew I wanted to go back to public service. And in comparison to what my mother earns and how I was raised, it's not modest at all. . . . I have no right to complain."[27]

CASELOAD

Not long after she arrived at Pearl Street, Sotomayor was added to what was known as "the wheel," which was a method for randomly selecting judges to hear new cases. In addition, Sotomayor received case files from other judges as the court attempted to distribute as equally as possible the caseload for each judge's docket. Sotomayor would then ask her clerks to review the case files, make notes, create memos, and schedule lawyers for each case to come in to confer with Sotomayor.

In the beginning, Sotomayor went very slowly, limiting her proceedings to conferences with lawyers who would meet in her office. As she stated later, "It was a little easier just to do my conferences in chambers and get used to having people call me judge." But it would be almost a year before Sotomayor felt comfortable in her new role and with her new title. "It's very strange to wear the title of 'Judge'," she remarked later, "Walking to the courthouse and having people call out to me 'Judge!' or having old friends not know whether to call me Sonia or Judge . . . has seemed strange to me. And defining those lines or drawing new lines or defining how I want my relationships to continue and with whom has been a difficult question during the year."[28]

As if dealing with caseloads and required reading was not enough, Sotomayor also had to keep up with current decisions of the Second Circuit Court of Appeals, which was the highest federal court operating in the state of New York. Clearly, Sotomayor wished to be as well prepared as possible in dealing with her cases; she expected no less from her clerks and the attorneys she worked with as well. Joseph Evall remembered how the judge would bring in the court decisions she had been up reading the night before. The pamphlets were underlined in pertinent places as well as filled with comments and notations. Sotomayor would hand them to her clerks, sometimes saying, "You're working on such and such an opinion; you should see this . . . She would grill lawyers about what the Second Circuit had just come down with. You did not want to be unprepared in her courtroom."[29]

During her time on the bench, Sotomayor would hear a number of notable cases involving everything from religious liberty to issues of privacy and security. For instance in 1993, she struck down as unconstitutional a law in White Plains, New York, that prohibited the displaying of a menorah in a park. The following year, Sotomayor, despite protests from officials, ruled that New York state prison inmates could wear beads of the Santeria religion under their belts. A 1995 ruling saw Sotomayor ordering the government to make public a photocopy of a torn-up note found in the briefcase of Vincent Foster, a former White House counsel under President Bill Clinton, who was thought to have committed suicide. In 1998, Sotomayor ruled that minimum wage was to be paid to the homeless people who worked for the Grand Central Partnership, a local business conglomerate. But by far, her most famous case came in 1995, when Sotomayor became to known as the savior of baseball.[30]

YOU'RE OUT!

At 9:45 P.M. on August 11, 1994, Seattle Mariners pitcher, Randy Johnson, struck out Oakland A's Ernie Young. That night, not just a baseball game ended, but the entire season ground to a halt, as baseball players walked off the field for what became the longest work stoppage in the history of major professional sports leagues in North America. As *Time* magazine commented:

> With that final, futile swing, the national pastime went down for the count as the more than 750 members of the Major League Players Association began their long-dreaded strike, baseball's eighth work stoppage since 1972. Never before have the games been halted this late in the season. Never before have the October play-offs and the World Series been in such dire jeopardy. Never before has the naked power struggle between players and owners seemed so heedless and self-destructive.[31]

The following seven months not only saw the cancellation of the World Series for the first time in 90 years, it also led to a mounting and acrimonious debate that threatened to sideline forever America's favorite pastime. The walkout, strike, and the resulting labor negotiations would be played out through bar room debates, meeting rooms in hotels, the federal courts, and even the White House. By the time the strike was resolved in 1995, the process had cost millions for baseball players and close to $1 billion for team owners. It would take an injunction from the federal court before fans would have an opportunity to hear an umpire call "play ball."[32]

According to baseball commissioner Bud Selig, the main issue over the strike was what he called competitive balance, that is, the idea that the big-market teams were dominating the small-market teams.

But anyone who had been following the ups and downs in relations between the players and management over the last several years knew that the root cause of the walkout was money. By the time of the walkout, the average player's salary was in the neighborhood of $1.2 million. The owners wanted a reduction in salaries and a salary cap, which they thought they could successfully force on the players. However, the player's association, led by Donald Fehr told Selig and management that the players wanted nothing to do with their demands. In addition, the players also did not want any more additional revenue sharing among the franchises, but did want a better benefits package. As Selig commented many years later of the strike, "It was tough. There was a lot of anger everywhere, particularly amongst our fans . . . It was the eighth work stoppage, so it had been building up for a long time. The sport came to a crashing halt."[33]

Negotiations between the players and the owners went on for months, with one side or the other angrily walking out on several occasions. Finally, on January 1, 1995, the United States Congress even got involved by introducing no fewer than five bills that tried to end the strike. However, nothing was resolved. On January 26, President Bill Clinton ordered the owners and players to resume bargaining. Even though both sides agreed to the president's request, nothing got accomplished. It was clear that the strike was now headed for the courts.[34]

The strike had every chance of continuing well into 1995. However, on March 27, the National Labor Relations Board accused the owners of unfair labor practices. Two days later, on March 29, the players agreed to return to work if a U.S. District Court Judge supported the complaint. The players got their wish: the judge chosen, a die-hard New York Yankees fan, was Sonia Sotomayor. The next day, on March 30, representatives from both sides found themselves in Judge Sotomayor's courtroom to make their arguments. As court convened, Sotomayor told the lawyers that, "I know nothing about this, except what a common layperson reads in the *New York Times* . . . I hope none of you assumed . . . that my lack of knowledge of any of the intimate details of your dispute meant that I was not a baseball fan. You can't grow up in the South Bronx without knowing about baseball."[35]

For the next two hours, Sotomayor grilled the attorneys. After hearing arguments from both sides, Sotomayor called for a 15-minute recess, after which Sotomayor told both parties she would have a decision about what to do. When the time was up, Sotomayor was ready: she ruled in favor of the players. Donald Fehr, who was acting as head attorney for the players' union later stated: "She obviously had done her homework well before the case was argued. . . . She was in control of her courtroom."[36]

Based on her findings, Sotomayor issued an injunction against the team owners telling them to restore free agency and arbitration. She also told the players that they needed to return to work. In the meantime, a new agreement was to be worked out. In her decision, Sotomayor took the owners to task stating, "The owners misunderstood the case law, and many of their arguments were inconsistent . . . One side can't come up with new rules unless they negotiate with the other." Sotomayor also stated that if she did not issue the injunction, "the harm to the players is the very one the owners' unfair labor practices sought to achieve, i.e., an alteration of free-agency rights and a skewing of their worth." In addition, Sotomayor wrote, "Issuing the injunction before opening day is important to ensure that the symbolic value of that day is not tainted by an unfair labor practice and the NLRB's inability to take effective steps against its perpetuation."[37]

REACTION

A few days after Sotomayor's ruling, a three-judge panel upheld her decision. And so it was on April 2, just 24 hours before the originally scheduled opening day, the baseball strike came to an end. It was decided that the 1995 season would be shortened to 144 games; on April 25, 1995, the first pitch of the season was thrown. Sotomayor's decision resonated with many people, especially in those areas with historically strong fan bases. The Philadelphia *Inquirer* wrote "that by saving the season, Judge Sotomayor joined forever the ranks of Joe DiMaggio, Willie Mays, Jackie Robinson and Ted Williams." The Chicago *Sun-Times* said she "delivered a wicked fastball" to baseball owners and emerged as one of the most inspiring figures in the history of the sport." The *New York Times* gushed: "U.S. District Judge Sonia Sotomayor in Manhattan did everything but sweep off the home plate and bellow, 'Play ball!' . . . Sotomayor did not need batting practice. She was the rare hitter who can 'wake up on Christmas Day and pull a curve ball,' as the old saying goes. She saw the stitches on the ball and she whacked it into the corner."[38]

However, not everyone was thrilled with the outcome of the baseball strike. Several sports columnists were offended by the speed in which Sotomayor delivered her verdict. Furman Bisher in the Atlanta *Journal Constitution* wrote, "I'm sorry she's not male, so I could say what I really think. I haven't the time or disposition to deal with NOW [the National Organization for Women] right now."

Noted conservative columnist and baseball aficionado George Will also found Sotomayor's decision troubling. According to Will, "What [Sotomayor] did was overturn in a sense, the essence, that underlies, the essential theory of American labor relations, which is the parties should slug it out because they know best and whoever wins, wins." Further, he wrote, "what she did was take sides, took union's side against the management, and in so-doing, wasted 262 days of negotiations. That, far from saving baseball, consigned baseball to seven more years of an unreformed economic system, which happened to be the seven worst years in terms of competitive balance." Will concluded, "far from her saving baseball . . . baseball thrives now because we got over the damage that her judicial activism did in that strike."[39]

However, the legal community overall supported Sotomayor's decision. Gary R. Roberts, the dean of the law school at Indiana University, called it the "right decision from a legal and tactical standpoint." Randy Levine, who became the owners' chief labor negotiator five months after Sotomayor's injunction, said her decision "gave both sides an opportunity to take a breath, to take stock of where they were. . . . It led to the good-faith bargaining that produced revenue sharing, the luxury tax and interleague play." Rick Karcher, a sports law professor probably summed up the contentious case best when he said, "It was the correct ruling."

NOTES

1. Wayne King, "Now, No Hispanic Candidates for Federal Bench in New York," *New York Times*, February 15, 1991, http://www.nytimes.com/1991/02/15/nyregion/now-no-hispanic-candidates-for-federal-bench-in-new-york.html?src=pm.

2. Ibid.

3. Ibid.

4. Campbell Gibson and Kay Jung, "Historical Census Statistics on Population Totals by Race, 1790 to 1990, and by Hispanic Origin, 1970 to 1990 for the United States, Regions, Divisions, and States, U.S. Census, Table 47. New York—Race and Hispanic Origin: 1790 to 1990," U.S. Census, http://www.census.gov/population/www/docu mentation/twps0056/tab47.pdf; "Latinos by Geography," Pew Hispanic Center, http://pewhispanic.org/states/population/.

5. King, "Now, No Hispanic Candidates for Federal Bench in New York."

6. Ibid.

7. Ibid.

8. Sheryl Gay Stolberg, "A Trailblazer and a Dreamer," *New York Times*, May 27, 2009: A1(L).

9. Ibid.

10. Michael Powell and Serge Kovaleski, "Sotomayor Rose on Merit Alone, Her Allies Say," *New York Times*, June 4, 2009, http://www.nytimes.com/2009/06/05/us/politics/05judge.html.

11. Ibid.

12. Neil A. Lewis, "On a Supreme Court Prospect's Resume: 'Baseball Savior'," *New York Times*, May 14, 2009, http://www.nytimes.com/2009/05/15/us/15sotomayor.html?ref=soniasotomayor; Lauren Collins, "Number Nine: Sonia Sotomayor's High Profile Debut," *New Yorker*, January 11, 2010, p. 49.

13. Ina R. Bort, "Judicial Profile: Hon. Sonia Sotomayor," *The Federal Lawyer* 53, no. 2 (February 2006), p. 37.

14. Lewis, "On a Supreme Court Prospect's Resume: 'Baseball Savior'."

15. Jason Horowitz, "The Many Rabbis of Sonia Sotomayor," *New York Observers Politicker NY*, May 26, 2009, http://www.observer.com/3719/many-rabbis-sonia-sotomayor.

16. Ibid.; Antonia Felix, *Sonia Sotomayor: The True American Dream*, New York: Berkeley Publishing Group, 2010, p. 152.

17. Felix, *Sonia Sotomayor*, p. 152.

18. Ibid.

19. "Confirmation Hearing on Hon. Susan Black, Sonia Sotomayor, Loretta Preska and Irene M. Keeley," U.S. Senate Committee

on the Judiciary, June 4, 1991, http://www.scotusblog.com/wp-content/uploads/2009/06/sotomayor-district-hearing.pdf.

20. Collins, "Number Nine: Sonia Sotomayor's High Profile Debut."

21. Felix, *Sonia Sotomayor,* p. 154; Collins, "Number Nine: Sonia Sotomayor's High Profile Debut."

22. Felix, *Sonia Sotomayor.*

23. Ibid., p. 155.

24. Ibid., p. 156.

25. Ibid., p. 157.

26. Jan Hoffman, "A Breakthrough Judge: What She Always Wanted," *New York Times,* September 25, 1992, B16.

27. Ibid.

28. Felix, *Sonia Sotomayor,* p. 157.

29. Ibid., p. 158.

30. Stolberg, "A Trailblazer and a Dreamer."

31. Walter Shapiro, John Dickerson, Janet I-Chin, David S. Jackson, "Bummer of '94," *Time,* August 22, 1994, http://www.time.com/time/magazine/article/0,9171,981283,00.html.

32. Associated Press, "1994 Strike as a Low Point for Baseball," *MLB-ESPN,* August 10, 2004, http://sports.espn.go.com/mlb/news/story?id=1856626.

33. Ibid.

34. Allen Barra, "Baseball's Costliest Walk," *Wall Street Journal,* October 28, 2009, http://online.wsj.com/article/SB100014240527487 04335904574497433535880354.html.

35. Sean Gregory, "How Sotomayor 'Saved' Baseball," *Time,* May 26, 2009, http://www.time.com/time/nation/article/0,8599,1900974,00.html.

36. Ibid.

37. Ibid.; Lewis, "On a Supreme Court Prospect's Resume: 'Baseball Savior'."

38. Gregory, "How Sotomayor 'Saved' Baseball"; George Vecsey, "Hope Comes to Baseball Just in Time," *New York Times,* April 1, 1995, p. 29.

39. Gregory, "How Sotomayor 'Saved' Baseball"; "Did Sotomayor Save Baseball?" *The Economist,* May 27, 2009, http://www.economist.com/blogs/democracyinamerica/2009/05/did_sotomayor_save_baseball.

Chapter 8

"AN OUTSTANDING HISPANIC WOMAN JUDGE"

It seemed by 1997 that Sonia Sotomayor had it all—a challenging job in the city she loved, friends and family to spend time with, and the daily surprises as a judge that kept her mind sharp and up-to-date on the most pressing legal issues of the day. She saw herself also as giving back to her community and in the process emerging as a strong role model for women, especially Latinas. Since her divorce from Kevin Noonan, Sotomayor had dated, but with her appointment to the bench, she announced to her friends that she would no longer be dating lawyers. As one friend later commented, Sotomayor's decision meant there would be fewer possibilities for potential dates. However, that did not stop her friend from setting up Sotomayor on a blind date.[1]

Thanks to her decision to end the baseball strike, Sotomayor also enjoyed a much higher public profile. Still as one newspaper article noted, "a judge, however, can occupy a lonely perch." As a friend remarked in the same article, the decision to become a judge is "a daunting, life-reordering decision. . . . It absolutely casts the rest of your life. And sure, it's scary." Added Judge Miriam Goldman Cedarbaum, who worked and socialized with Sotomayor, "We are more isolated than at a law firm. . . . You still have good friendships, but it's a different world."[2]

BREAKING THE CEILING

Sotomayor may have grown comfortable with her role as a judge on the federal bench, but she was not prepared for the gender bias that she encountered while working at the Federal Courthouse on Pearl Street. If anything, the situations she experienced were even worse than anything she had seen since she began practicing law and was working at the DA's office and in private practice. More than once, she was waylaid by male attorneys in court who attempted to give her advice. These paternalistic overtures became a regular pattern in her courtroom, no matter what she did to dissuade the attorneys from giving her advice in her courtroom.

Sotomayor had few illusions of the gender bias present in the legal field. She also knew that as a woman, she had to work twice as hard in order to be taken as seriously as her male colleagues. Still the reality of her and other women lawyers' situation was a frustrating one. In a very early (1986) interview with *Mademoiselle*, a popular women's magazine, Sotomayor remarked, "it's not that I feel I've been discriminated against as a woman, but I've had to devote so much extra time to overcompensating for my gender—time I could have put to use in more productive ways." She went on: "I've noticed that if you're a woman you have to work twice as hard, be twice as good. The doors do eventually open, but sometimes it's just so daunting to get them to open. I've had to face that fact that I could probably never be president—not because I'm Puerto Rican, but because I'm a woman. I've come to seriously doubt whether I'll ever see a woman president in my lifetime, and that's very, very disappointing."[3]

Still, Sotomayor had her own ways at circumventing gender bias. For many years, she hid the fact that she could type. Her law clerk Joe Evall stated, "She had always pretended that she didn't know how to type because she didn't want to be relegated to the role of the note taker. . . . It is easy in a lot of work environments to make the woman the note taker, and she was very savvy about that." Sotomayor also challenged conventional dress codes of the 1980s and 1990s by wearing a pants suit under her judicial robes. Evall later stated that he told the judge that her wardrobe choice sent an important message to all people, but particularly women, in that it was an "OK wardrobe for people in a legal work environment. . . . By doing it she was saying, 'This is what I'm wearing, let people get used to it.' If the judge is doing it, it sends a message."[4]

CARVING OUT A LIFE

When not hearing cases or working in her chambers, Sotomayor worked hard at creating a more balanced life. She continued to travel and also made the most of the many cultural offerings of New York City: attending symphonies, concerts, museums and of course, ball games. She stated, "I realized I needed to strike a balance. . . . I still want to be successful, but I also want to be happy and not sacrifice personal satisfaction for an intellectual one. All my life I've worked so hard I've never learned to enjoy life. Now I'm learning."[5]

That learning took on many different shapes. In her office, Sotomayor worked hard to create a friendly atmosphere with her staff. Often the group would eat lunch ordered in from any variety of restaurants in the area. Sotomayor, her secretary, and law clerks would chat about television, sports, or other topics. She considered her clerks and secretary her work family and enjoyed warm relationships with all. Her warmth extended throughout the courthouse where on any given day, Sotomayor would stop and greet the court's clerks, court reporters, marshals, judges, and attorneys she would meet in the halls. As one of her clerks, Xavier Romeu, later recalled, those walks through the courthouse turned "into a seemingly endless progression of smiles, gestures and conversations . . . that . . . always went beyond mere pleasantries, beyond courthouse business or shallow observations."[6]

Even though Sotomayor was still interested in dating, she had ruled out the possibility of ever having children, in part because of her diabetes and because she knew how driven she was to succeed in her legal career. Instead she turned her energies to the nephews and nieces in her family as well her godchildren. Sotomayor continued to successfully manage her diabetes, a not-so-small-feat given the stresses of her career. She was known for her small black pouch that went with her everywhere and that contained a blood sugar testing kit, a needle, and insulin. She was not shy about having to use it in front of people when necessary. "She'll be eating Chinese dumplings and she'll say, 'Excuse me sweetie,' and pull out the kit and inject her insulin," said Xavier Romeu. Unlike many diabetics who prefer to wear pumps that deliver a metered dose of insulin, Sotomayor preferred to give herself injections much as she did as a small child in the Bronxdale Houses many years ago. It was testimony to her determination not to let the disease dictate her life as well as her watchful discipline over her condition that led her doctor to comment that her blood sugar levels were better than 98 percent of diabetics. Sotomayor also was free from other complications that come from the disease such as eye, kidney, and nerve damage.[7]

The threat of a short life because of her diabetes seemed to be receding too. "Sonia told me many years ago that because of her diabetes, she had only a certain amount of time to live," said Toni Smith, who worked with Sotomayor in the Manhattan DA's office. "She's lived maybe 20 years longer than she ever thought she would." Another close friend added that Sotomayor takes special care to watch what she ate and took the best care of herself possible, "but not in a way that makes her a victim of a disease or a person whose life is ruled by a disease."[8]

NOMINATION

On June 25, 1997, Judge Sonia Sotomayor received a phone call: on the other end of the phone was the then-president of the United States, Bill Clinton, who called to offer Sotomayor an appointment to the Second Circuit Court of Appeals. The court was the second highest court in the land, surpassed only by the Supreme Court. Clinton's offer also belied something that her mentor Senator Daniel Moynihan spotted many years ago: the potential to one day sit on the bench as a Supreme Court Justice. An appointment such as this to the Circuit Court suggested that the president also considered Sotomayor a possible contender one day for the Supreme Court.[9]

The United States Court of Appeals was created in 1891. The duty of the court is to provide intermediate review of cases that come to the district courts but have not been advanced to the Supreme Court. Because the Supreme Court hears so few cases, the Court of Appeals is usually the last stop for many people whose cases are seeking another chance. The Second Circuit Court is one of 13 Courts of Appeals in the United States, and is probably the best-known court of all. The

Second Court's territory consists of the states of Connecticut, New York, and Vermont; the court also had jurisdiction over district courts in selected areas of those three states. The court consists of 12 active judges and 12 senior judges. In the case of the Second Circuit Court, the decisions made are binding on the lower district courts of their particular area. To sit as a judge on this appellate court was a very powerful position within the judicial framework of the United States.[10]

Serving on the appellate court would be a dramatic change for Sotomayor. Unlike the trial court atmosphere of the Southern Court, Sotomayor would be considering the legal arguments of a decision that came before her. There would be no trial, no jury, and no looking at evidence in making a decision. Instead, she would be one of three appellate court judges who would review legal briefs and hear arguments from lawyers for both sides. Decisions would be based on those arguments on whether to uphold the previous judgment or to overturn it.

If the appellate court overturned a decision, the litigants had the opportunity to present their case to the Supreme Court, but whether their case would be heard would be at the court's discretion. After considering what lay before her, Sotomayor made her decision to accept the president's offer.

At the time, it appeared that Sotomayor's nomination would be a problem-free choice for Clinton, whose administration had been rocked by a host of problems and controversies almost from the beginning. Her background story would surely resonate with many people. Her legal experience showed her to be a dedicated lawyer and thoughtful jurist. What also appeared to be another plus was the fact that she had been appointed to the federal bench under a republican president, which could preempt any potential problems with partisan politics in securing her nomination and appointment.

START AND STOP

As soon as the announcement was made that Sonia Sotomayor was to President Clinton's pick for the empty seat on the Second Circuit Court, Sotomayor's supporters stepped up. Both New York Senators Moynihan and D'Amato as well as numerous lawyers and various organizations wrote letters to the U.S. Senate Judiciary Committee expressing their support for the president's candidate. A group from the Puerto Rican Bar Association was among the first of many to speak to the Senate Committee on Sotomayor's behalf. Even the governor of Puerto Rico, Pedro Ronsello endorsed Sotomayor's nomination. In addition, the American Bar Association, upon reviewing her record voted and gave Sotomayor its highest rating of well-qualified.[11]

Things appeared to be moving along until one morning in June, Sotomayor picked up a copy of *The Wall Street Journal* and read the paper's editorial stating that she was a left-leaning judge. In particular, the paper took issue with two of her rulings: *Archie v. Grand Central Partnership* (1998) in which she required a business consortium to pay its homeless workers minimum wage and *Marilyn Bartlett v. New York State Board of Law Examiners* (1995) in which Sotomayor ordered the New York Bar Association to accommodate a law student suffering from dyslexia by offering the student more time to take the test as well as allowing the student to take the exam by computer. Adding more fuel to the fire was conservative radio talk-show host Rush Limbaugh's picking up on the news item and broadcasting it to his radio audience. "Unfortunately, at 12 noon of the day of my hearing, Rush Limbaugh decided to devote his radio show to my nomination," Sotomayor recalled later. Limbaugh's objections were strategic: Sotomayor was on a "rocket ship" to the Supreme Court, he warned his listeners.[12]

What had earlier seemed a fairly straightforward nomination and appointment now appeared to be headed for the rocks. As Limbaugh had warned, some Republicans were convinced that Clinton was promoting Sotomayor to the Second Circuit Court in order to better position her for a future spot on the Supreme Court bench. However, as one article pointed out: "Several elements of the Sotomayor case are odd, White House officials and Democrats in Congress say, but the chief one is the fact that there is no vacancy on the Supreme Court, and no firm indication that there will be one soon. Nor is there any evidence of a campaign to put Judge Sotomayor under consideration for a seat if there were a vacancy."

What was clear was that any delay of Sotomayor's confirmation illustrated the growing partisanship and the increasingly difficult byzantine political maneuverings that had become a staple of modern-day judicial nominations.[13]

By 1997 and 1998, the problem of bipartisanship had taken a tremendous toll on the appointment of judges to a number of empty slots
on federal benches across the country. In addressing the situation in
September 1997 at Sotomayor's nomination hearings, Senator Patrick
Leahy (D-Vermont) stated:

> This year the Senate has confirmed only 11 federal judges, during
> a period in which we have seen 112 vacancies. We have two nom-
> inees from the June 25 hearings who still need to be considered
> and reported by the Judiciary Committee and nominees pending
> on the Senate Executive calendar from as long ago as June 12.
>
> This is only the fifth confirmation hearing for judicial nomi-
> nees that this Committee has held all year. From the first days of
> this session of Congress, this Committee has never had pending
> before it fewer than 20 judicial nominees for hearings. This Com-
> mittee's backlog has now doubled and is more than 40. Many of
> these nominations, pending for longer than a year, have been re-
> nominated by the President after having been held up during the
> stall last year. . . . And while I am delighted to see the Committee
> moving forward promptly on nominations received at the end of
> July, that does not excuse us for having passed over and not held
> hearings on dozens of other nominees throughout the year. The
> Committee has 12 nominations that have been pending for more
> than a year, including seven nominations that have been pending
> since 1995 . . .
>
> Chief Justice Rehnquist has repeatedly acknowledged the crisis
> being inflicted upon the federal judiciary and, I believe, upon all
> Americans. The Chief Justice has called the rising number of va-
> cancies "the most immediate problem we face in the federal judi-
> ciary." . . . The effect is seen in extended delay in the hearing and
> determination of cases and the frustration that litigants are forced
> to endure. The crushing caseload will force federal courts to rely
> more and more on senior judges, visiting judges and court staff.[14]

Leahy even read the text of a presidential radio message from Clinton
into the record. In his message, Clinton clearly showed his dismay over
the manner in which his nominees for the judiciary had been treated:

In the past 18 months this vital partnership has broken down as the Senate has refused to act on nomination after nomination. And in federal courthouses across America, almost 100 judges' benches are empty. In 1996, the Senate confirmed just 17 judges—that's the lowest election-year total in over 40 years. This year I've already sent 70 nominations to Congress, but so far they've acted on less than 20. The result is a vacancy crisis in our courts. . . . Meanwhile, our courts are clogged with a rising number of cases. An unprecedented number of civil cases are stalled, affecting the lives of tens of thousands of Americans—from the family seeking life insurance proceeds, to the senior citizen trying to collect Social Security benefits, to the small business protecting its right to compete. In our criminal courts nearly 16,000 cases are caught in limbo, while criminals on bail await punishment and victims await justice. Our sitting judges are overloaded and overworked, and our justice system is strained to the breaking point.

The Senate's failure to act on my nominations, or even to give many of my nominees a hearing, represents the worst of partisan politics. Under the pretense of preventing so-called judicial activism, they've taken aim at the very independence our founders sought to protect. The congressional leadership has actually threatened sitting judges with impeachment, merely because it disagrees with their judicial opinions. Under this politically motivated scrutiny, under ever-mounting caseloads, our judges must struggle to enforce the laws Congress passes and to do justice for us all. We can't let partisan politics shut down our courts and gut our judicial system. I've worked hard to avoid that. And the people I've nominated for judgeships and had confirmed have had the highest rating of well qualified from the American Bar Association of any President since these ratings have been kept. So today I call upon the Senate to fulfill its constitutional duty to fill these vacancies. The intimidation, the delay, the shrill voices must stop so the unbroken legacy of our strong, independent judiciary can continue.[15]

FACING THE PANEL

In September 1997, the Senate Judiciary Committee began its questioning of Sotomayor. One of her strongest supporters, Senator Alfonse

D'Amato, recognized Sotomayor and described her many accomplishments in glowing terms:

> As it relates to Justice Sotomayor, what can one say but "only in this country." The daughter of a humble working family has risen by way of her legal, scholastic stewardship to the highest trial court in the federal district, and premier district I might add with some prejudice. Of the Southern District of New York where she has distinguished herself. And I predicted to this committee, almost five years ago, that Judge Sotomayor would be an exemplary, outstanding justice. . . . Her experience, both as a prosecutor, civil litigator, and federal trial judge, makes her an exceptionally qualified candidate for the Second Circuit.[16]

Sotomayor was asked a variety of questions ranging from her interpretations of the Constitution, her reasons for particular court decisions, and her opinions on the federal sentencing guidelines. All the questions had elements of controversy about them. However, Sotomayor faced each question squarely with careful consideration and measure; her answers were clear and forthright. For instance, when Senator Strom Thurmond posed a question about federal sentence guidelines, Sotomayor used the opportunity to explain how society imposes its views on the crime, rather than the judge:

> Senator Thurmond: Another question. Some argue that the Federal sentencing guidelines do not provide enough flexibility for the sentencing judge and some even say they should be abolished. What is your view of the Federal sentencing guidelines, based on your experience with them?
>
> Judge Sotomayor: Thus far, sir, in the vast majority of cases, I have found the guidelines to be very helpful in giving some comfort to me as a judge that I am not arbitrarily imposing sentences based on my personal feelings. I believe that congressional sentiment, as reflected in the guidelines, is important because it permits me not to impose my personal views but to let the democracy impose the society's views. With respect to your second point. Senator, the guidelines already provide mechanisms for departures in appropriate circumstances. In my experience, when there are principled and reasoned grounds to depart, the guidelines already permit it.[17]

However, not everyone was inclined to admire Sotomayor for her ac-complishments. Senator Jeff Sessions (R-Ala.) mentioned rumors that she refused to stand when Supreme Court Justice Clarence Thomas addressed a 1992 meeting with Second Circuit judges. The exchange underscored the tension and resentment on the part of conservative Republicans over Sotomayor's nomination. According to the testi-mony transcripts, Senator Sessions demanded to know whether Soto-mayor gave Justice Thomas the proper respect:

Senator Sessions: One more thing. I noticed a *New York Times* ar-ticle that indicated that you had not applauded or not stood and applauded when Justice Thomas appeared at the second circuit conference. Are you aware of that?

Judge Sotomayor: Well, I never did say that, sir. I took the fifth amendment when the *New York Times* asked me that because of the raging controversy at the time. I thought it made no sense for a prospective nominee to enter that kind of political fray by any statement, but I do not think I ever did, sir.

Senator Sessions: Well, that might explain it. The question in the article was, when Justice Clarence Thomas was introduced at the second circuit conference, the question of the reporter was, were you among those who sat on her hands rather than giving him a standing ovation, and you said, "I will take the Fifth."

Judge Sotomayor: I explained to her clearly, as I do to you now, I did that because I thought as a—at that point, I was a confirmed nominee, and as a judge, that I should never be making political statements to the press or anyone else and I thought that was a politically charged question.

Senator Sessions: Let me just ask you, did you see fit to stand and applaud when he was introduced?

Judge Sotomayor: He was my Supreme Court Justice of my cir-cuit. I stood up.[18]

STALLED OUT

Sotomayor appeared to get through the hearings unscathed. However, it was not until March 1998, before the Judiciary Committee finally cast their votes, 16–2, to send Sotomayor's name to the full Senate for confirmation. Casting votes against her were Senate Republicans John Ashcroft of Missouri and John Kyl of Arizona. The committee's other conservative Republicans including Orrin G. Hatch of Utah and Strom Thurmond of South Carolina, voted for Sotomayor. One newspaper article noted that "Of the judicial nominees who have cleared the committee in this Congress, she [Sotomayor] is among those who have waited the longest for a final vote on the floor."[19]

Clearly, Senate Republicans were taking to heart the possibility of Clinton naming Sotomayor to a vacancy on the Supreme Court, particularly in light of the impending resignation of Justice John Paul Stevens from the bench, though Stevens had not given a firm date and had even gone as far as hiring law clerks for the next session. One staff aide for Trent Lott of Mississippi, the then-majority leader of the Senate stated: "Basically, we think that putting her on the appeals court puts her in the batter's box to be nominated to the Supreme Court. . . . If Clinton nominated her it would put several of our senators in a real difficult position." Many Republicans believed that Sotomayor was what was euphemistically called an activist judge, that is, one who interprets the law narrowly. It is a description that Sotomayor's supporters took issue with, including Senator Patrick Leahy of Vermont, the senior Democrat on the Judiciary Committee, who bluntly remarked that the Republicans' "reasons are stupid at best and cowardly at worst. What they are saying is that they have a brilliant judge who also happens to be a woman and Hispanic, and they haven't the guts to stand up and argue publicly against her on the floor. . . . They just want to hide in their cloakrooms and do her in quietly."[20]

This strategy for positioning justices on appeals courts so they can eventually be moved to the Supreme Court was nothing new. The Republicans tried it with nominees Judge Robert H. Bork, whose nomination was defeated in 1987, and Judge Clarence Thomas who was confirmed in 1991. In both the cases, the nominees faced bruising and brutal confirmation hearings by the Senate Judiciary Committee that also underscored the growing levels of acrimony between conservative Republicans and liberal Democrats.[21]

Some on Capitol Hill found the Republicans' thinking at best speculative and at worst, misinformed. In part, the Republicans were basing their strategy of stopping Sotomayor's nomination on the idea that President Clinton was hoping to make the first Hispanic appointment to the Supreme Court. The Republicans were also not taking into consideration the fact that even though Hispanic legal organizations and groups had been pressing Clinton's administration to naming a Hispanic Supreme Court Justice, the White House never definitively stated it would do so. By 1998, the Hispanic National Bar Association had submitted to the White House a list of six viable candidates for the Supreme Court. Missing from that list? Sonia Sotomayor.[22]

CONFIRMED

Finally, in October 1998, under relentless pressuring from Hispanic groups, which included the writing of thousands of letters to senators from all over the country, Sotomayor's nomination finally made it to the Senate floor. She was confirmed, 67–29 as a Judge to the Second Circuit Court of Appeals. On November 9, her installation was held at the federal courthouse on Pearl Street, where only a few years earlier, she had been first appointed to the bench. At the ceremony, Sotomayor was surrounded by her family, friends, and supporters, including Senator Moynihan, Robert Morgenthau, former and present law clerks and members of various Puerto Rican organizations. The oath of office was given to Sotomayor by her mentor at Yale, José Cabranes, now a judge with the Second Circuit. Also in attendance was another judge from the Second Circuit, Guido Calbresi, who taught Sotomayor at Yale.[23]

There was another person present at the ceremony who held a special place in Sotomayor's life: building contractor Peter White, with whom Sotomayor had fallen in love. The two had met in 1994 and had been inseparable since then. White, like Sotomayor, had grown up in the Bronx; he was a dapper figure who loved the outdoors. One friend of Sotomayor's commented in a profile of Sotomayor that while White was not a match for Sotomayor's intellect, he was smart, convivial, and looked good in a tuxedo. White was also not overwhelmed by her reputation. By the time of Sotomayor's confirmation, the couple were engaged and living together. They hoped to be married sometime after Sotomayor's Senate confirmation.[24]

Sotomayor paid a special tribute to the man in her life during her induction speech when she turned to White and said, "Peter, you have made me a whole person, filling not just the voids of emptiness that existed before you, but making me a better, a more loving and a more generous person. Many of my closest friends forget just how emotionally withdrawn I was before I met you." When her speech was over, White helped her slip on her appellate judges robe. Unfortunately, Sotomayor's happiness would not last. Less than two years later, after she gave a party at their newly renovated apartment for his 50th birthday, the couple's relationship ended. White moved to Westchester County, bought a small boat and married a woman who was an acquaintance of Sotomayor's and who was 14 years the judge's junior. The dissolution of the relationship was not easy for Sotomayor. As one friend later commented, "It was very tough on Sonia."[25]

After her appointment, Sotomayor should have been ecstatic. But her treatment at the hands of the press, the Judiciary Committee, and the Senate Republicans had stung. Sotomayor was resentful at what she perceived as Republican stereotypes of her: that because she was a woman, she was a liberal, and a bleeding heart liberal at that. She later commented, "Although we all wish to believe that appointments are only the product of merit, the harsh reality is that the support of community groups is critical to insuring that meritorious candidates are not overlooked or victimized in the appointment process . . . stereotyping is perhaps the most insidious of all problems in our society today."[26]

TO WORK

Sotomayor's chambers were now located at the federal courthouse on Foley Square in New York City. Life quickly settled into a routine. Sotomayor still spent a lot of time reading briefs, a practice that many judges pass on. She then would pass the documents and her comments on to her clerks who were to research her notes. Many of her clerks were struck by the degree of information Sotomayor required from lower court rulings. "She takes each case and works it to death to get the right result," Adam Abensohn, a former clerk, described how Sotomayor would look at each legal case and study it from every angle until

Federal Judge Sonia Sotomayor poses by her office window in New York overlooking the old Federal Court- house on Foley Square in 1998. (AP Photo/Mark Lennihan, FILE)

she was satisfied with her decision. Danielle Tarantolo, another former clerk, said that Sotomayor has an unusual ability to isolate the pressure points of a case.[27]

She was no different in the courtroom, where preparation was key to staying on the judge's good side. Criminal-defense attorney Gerald Shargel recalled, "She can be, and is, won over by lawyers who are pre- pared. But if a lawyer acts like a fool she will go for the jugular." Nor did her clerks find Sotomayor to be the stereotypical liberal judge that con- servative Republicans warned about. One former clerk stated, "People who think she's going to be a really reliable liberal on all issues—I don't know! But people simplify. No one is harder on prosecutors. If you . . . withhold Brady info (evidence that is favorable to a defendant) or do something that's unethical or wrong, she will destroy you." Soto- mayor might bend sentencing guidelines, as in the case where a police officer had been found guilty of selling heroin. Although the probation report recommended four to five years in prison, Sotomayor, stated that the former office had abused the trust of his position and sentenced him to seven years. At the same time, Sotomayor showed she was a strict disciplinarian for procedural safeguards of the law, making sure that criminals have full benefits of due process in their cases.[28]

Like Pearl Street, Sotomayor tried to create a friendly atmosphere with her clerks and secretary. Sotomayor could be a demanding task-master, but she also knew it was important for her people to be able to relax and have fun. When the popular film "Harry Potter and the Order of the Phoenix," arrived at New York theaters, Sotomayor took everyone to the movies during a workday. One Halloween, Sotomayor decorated the office with scarecrows and pumpkins; for the holidays, she brought in both Christmas decorations and a menorah.[29]

During the 2006–2007 term, after she had spent a long and tiring day of interviewing potential clerks to fill in for the next year, Soto-mayor decided to invite her current clerks to her Greenwich apartment where they feasted on hamburgers and drank beer. Kyle Wong, a former clerk, recalled how the judge sat with her clerks playing Texas hold 'em until two o'clock in the morning. When the evening's festivities had concluded, Sotomayor made sure everyone had cab fare and sent her crew off, telling them not to come into the office before 10 A.M. to give them time to recuperate from the evening's festivities.[30]

NOTABLE CASES

One area in which Sotomayor was seen as being more liberal in her de-cisions was in cases regarding immigration. Bruno Bembi, a lawyer who argued several immigration cases before Sotomayor, stated in a *New Yorker* profile piece that Sotomayor was amiable to interpretations of the law that allowed immigrants some leeway if those arguments were reasonable in scope and presentation. Judge Rosemary Pooler, who also sat on the Sec-ond Circuit, stated that she found Sotomayor willing to work at finding the right solution within an increasingly complex and rigid system that would allow immigrants to seek and find asylum in the United States.[31]

One example of this was in the case *Lin v. United States Department of Justice* (2007), in which three Chinese aliens, who were unmarried partners of women who had been subject to China's forced-abortion policies, petitioned for automatic asylum to the United States on the basis of persecution. Their claim was rejected by the majority of the Second Circuit, with the judges stating that automatic asylum did not extend to spouses or to unmarried partners. Sotomayor's opinion disputed the rulings showing not only a concern about the legal issues, but the human consequences as well. In her opinion, since the petitioners were unmarried, the court had erred, in considering the question of whether partners and spouses should be permitted asylum and further, that the court should have recognized that spouses can experience persecution by association: "The termination of a wanted pregnancy under a coercive population control program can only be devastating to any couple, akin, no doubt, to the killing of a child."

In writing her opinions, Sotomayor considered herself an average writer and that words are a means, not an end in putting together a legal decision. As one clerk noted, "She writes for people who want to know what the law is." Another clerk summed it up this way: "She believes that this is a serious business we're doing, and a judge shouldn't be taking the time to write a novel." For Sotomayor, legal opinions were little more than instruction manuals in how to apply the law. To that end, everyone should be able to understand what is being said. One example of this was in the case *Farrell v. Burke* (2006), in which Sotomayor instead of writing a treatise on the First Amendment, simply chose to include the following exchange from the testimony of a police officer who charged a convicted sex offender for violating the terms of his probation by possessing pornography:

Mr. Nathanson:	Are you saying, for example, that that condition of parole would prohibit Mr. Farrell from possessing, say, *Playboy* magazine?
P.O. Burke:	Yes.
Mr. Nathanson:	Are you saying that that condition of parole would prohibit Mr. Farrell from possessing a photograph of Michelangelo['s] *David*?
P.O. Burke:	What is that?
Mr. Nathanson:	Are you familiar with that sculpture?
P.O. Burke:	No.
Mr. Nathanson:	If I tell you it's a large sculpture of a nude youth with his genitals exposed and visible, does that help to refresh your memory of what that is?
P.O. Burke:	If he possessed that, yes, he would be locked up for that.[32]

Sotomayor ruled that Farrell had violated his parole. She wrote, "Although a series of strongly worded opinions by this Court and others suggest that the term 'pornography' is unconstitutionally vague, we hold that Scum [magazine] falls within any reasonable definition of pornography."[33]

In the case Ford v. McGinnis (2003), Sotomayor tackled the issue of free speech in which she reversed the decision of a district court that a Muslim prisoner's free-exercise rights had not been violated when he was refused a meal for the feast of Eid al Fitr. In the case of Hayden v. Pataki (2006), she also used a literal reading of the Voting Rights Act to argue that felons should be allowed to contest their disenfranchisement, even though by law they are unable to vote.[34]

"Sonia's tendency has been to suffer evils until she deems them no longer sufferable," stated Peter Kougasian, one of Sotomayor's Princeton classmates and former colleague in the Manhattan DA's office. Clearly Sotomayor was emerging as a justice who weighed her decisions carefully and tried to achieve as balanced a judgment as possible that took into account the law and human nature. She showed herself to be a passionate advocate of those who could not defend themselves, particularly in her dissents, such as the 2004 case N.G. and S.G. v. Connecticut (2004), in which she objected to the strip search of girls at juvenile-detention centers and in the case of Gant v. Wallingford Board of Education (1999), where Sotomayor defended an African American first grader, the only black in his class who was moved back to kindergarten only after nine days.[35]

FUTURE POSSIBILITIES?

Even though Sotomayor was showing herself to be an able jurist who followed her own conscience, she was still dogged by detractors, who found her "sharp-tongued and possessed with an occasionally combative manner" and hard to deal with both in and out of the courtroom. Some critics went so far as to call her "difficult" and "nasty," raising questions about her capacity to judge effectively. Her temperament was cause of concern to allies and enemies alike who saw Sotomayor in the position of becoming a potential Supreme Court nominee.[36]

Both Sotomayor's colleagues and attorneys who have come before her found her style to be assertive. Sotomayor was known to run what was called a "hot bench," that is, a courtroom where the judge asks lawyers a lot of questions. H. Raymond Fasano, an immigration lawyer who appeared before Sotomayor numerous times stated, "When a judge asks a lot of questions, that means she's read the record, she knows the issues and she has concerns that she wants resolved. And that's the judge's job." At the same time, Sotomayor was also known to send to attorneys very detailed memorandums critiquing their draft opinions.

Other lawyers were not convinced. According to the *Almanac of the Federal Judiciary*, which conducts anonymous interviews with lawyers to evaluate judges, Sotomayor's reviews dropped from enthusiastic to tepid. Among the comments about her were that she was a "terror on the bench" who "behaves in an out-of-control manner" and attacks lawyers "for making an argument she doesn't like." Sheema Chaudhry, an attorney who appeared before Sotomayor charged that she "could be very judgmental in the sense that she doesn't let you finish your argument before she jumps in and starts asking questions . . . She's brilliant and she's qualified, but I just feel that she can be very, how do you say, temperamental."[37]

Gerald Lefcourt, a New York defense lawyer who has known Sotomayor since she was an assistant DA found her "more strident and much more vocal" than the other judges when he came before her in the Second Circuit Court. "She used her questioning to make a point," he said, "as opposed to really looking for an answer to a question she did not understand." Judge Guido Calabresi, Sotomayor's former professor and now colleague on the bench dismissed the complaints about his former student as sour grapes. Calabresi said in a *New York Times* article that her behavior was no different than that of his male colleagues. "Some lawyers just don't like to be questioned by a woman," he added.[38]

By election year 2008, Sotomayor had been on the bench for 16 years. Despite disappointments in her personal life, she had established herself as a formidable jurist. She had received a number of honorary degrees recognizing her service to the legal profession and to the community: in 2001, Princeton awarded her an honorary doctorate, and in 2007 it named her as a trustee to the university. She also received honors from Brooklyn Law School, Lehman College of the City University of New York, Northeastern University School of Law, and Pace

University Law School. In a commencement speech to Pace University graduates, Sotomayor said:

> I love my work. It stimulates and challenges me. I wake up each morning excited about the prospect of engaging in work that fulfills me and gives me a chance to have a voice in the development of law. I love the law—I admire our profession for all the good it has and continues to do in the world. I respect the rule of law because it helps us as communities of people organize ourselves into civilized patterns of human behavior. Even when the rule of law fails, as some may consider it has in some of the events of recent times, we still look to it for comfort and a sense of security. It gives us much and I am eternally grateful that I am a member of a noble profession. . . . It is a very rare blessing when one can live ones professional dreams as completely as I have been able to.[39]

But Sotomayor's career still was on the rise. Little did she, or many others, realize how historic 2008's election would be. And with that election and the nation's new president, Sonia Sotomayor stood poised to make history once more.

NOTES

1. Lauren Collins, "Number Nine: Sonia Sotomayor's High Profile Debut," *New Yorker*, January 11, 2010, p. 50.

2. Michael Powell, "To Get to Sotomayor's Core, Go to New York," *New York Times*, July 9, 2009, http://www.nytimes.com/2009/07/10/nyregion/10sonia.html?pagewanted=all.

3. Catherine Lawson, "A Touch of Class," *Mademoiselle*, September 1986, p. 257.

4. Antonia Felix, *Sonia Sotomayor: The True American Dream*, New York: Berkeley Publishing Group, 2010, p. 183.

5. Felix, *Sonia Sotomayor*, p. 186.

6. Ibid.

7. Sheryl Gay Stolberg, "Court Nominee Manages Diabetes with Discipline," *New York Times*, July 9, 2009, http://www.nytimes.com/2009/07/10/us/politics/10diabetes.html.

8. Ibid.

9. Greg B. Smith, "Judges Journey to Top Bronx' Sotomayor Rose from Projects to Court of Appeals," *Daily News*, October 24, 1998, p. 17.

10. "Second Circuit Court," Federal Judicial Center, http://www.fjc.gov/history/home.nsf/page/courts_of_appeals.html.

11. Felix, *Sonia Sotomayor,* p. 189.

12. Neil A. Lewis, "G.O.P., Its Eyes on High Court, Blocks a Judge," *New York Times*, June 13, 1998, A1; Collins, "Number Nine: Sonia Sotomayor's High Profile Debut."

13. Collins, "Number Nine: Sonia Sotomayor's High Profile Debut."

14. "Hearings Before the Committee on the Judiciary, United States Senate, September 5, 30, October 28, 29, November 12, 1997," http://www.archive.org/stream/confirmationhear972unit/confirmationhear972unit_djvu.txt.

15. Ibid.

16. Ibid.

17. Ibid.

18. Ibid.

19. Lewis, "G.O.P., Its Eyes on High Court, Blocks a Judge."

20. Ibid.

21. Ibid.

22. Ibid.

23. Ibid.; Felix, *Sonia Sotomayor,* p. 196.

24. Collins, "Number Nine: Sonia Sotomayor's High Profile Debut," p. 50.

25. Powell, "To Get to Sotomayor's Core, Go to New York."

26. Smith, "Judges Journey to Top Bronx' Sotomayor Rose from Projects to Court of Appeals."

27. Collins, "Number Nine: Sonia Sotomayor's High Profile Debut," p. 49.

28. Ibid.

29. Ibid., p. 50.

30. Ibid.

31. Ibid.

32. "Sotomayor's Porn Trial," *Atlantic*, June 1, 2009, http://www.theatlantic.com/daily-dish/archive/2009/06/sotomayors-porn-trial/201114/.

33. Collins, "Number Nine: Sonia Sotomayor's High Profile Debut," p. 51.

34. Ibid.

35. Ibid., p. 50.

36. Jo Becker and Adam Liptak, "Sotomayor's Blunt Style Raises Issue of Temperament," *New York Times*, May 28, 2009, http://www.nytimes.com/2009/05/29/us/politics/29judge.html?pagewanted=all.

37. Ibid.

38. Ibid.

39. Sonia Sotomayor, "Pace Law School Honorary Degree Acceptance Speech," May 18, 2003, http://www.law.pace.edu/files/com mencement/honorarydegree/SotomayorSpeech05182003.pdf.

Chapter 9

A HISTORIC CHOICE

Obama Chooses Sotomayor for High Court

May 26, 2009

President Obama on Tuesday nominated U.S. Circuit Judge Sonia Sotomayor to serve on the Supreme Court, tapping the daughter of Puerto Rican parents to succeed retiring Justice David Souter and become the first Hispanic to serve on the high court.

Calling Sotomayor "an inspiring woman," Obama said that he looked not only at intellect and the ability to be impartial, but at life experience and the ability to relate to ordinary Americans in choosing Sotomayor as his nominee.

At a White House news conference, Sotomayor thanked the president for "the most humbling honor" of her life. "My heart today is bursting with gratitude," she said.

If confirmed by the Senate, the 54-year-old judge will bring nearly 17 years of experience on the federal bench and a history of bipartisan appeal to the high court. She was first appointed to federal bench in the Southern District of New York in 1992 by President

George H.W. Bush and was named to the 2nd Circuit Court of Appeals by President Bill Clinton in 1998. . . . Republicans are not expected to put up much of a fight against the nomination.[1]

MAKING HEADLINES

In late April 2009, Sonia Sotomayor was on her way to the gym for a workout when she received a phone call. On the phone was a staff member calling on behalf of the newly elected President Barack Obama. The aide told Sotomayor that the White House Legal Counsel Office was trying to get in touch with her. Sotomayor took down the phone number and promised to get in touch as soon as she could. When she called the Legal Counsel Office, she was told that there would soon be a resignation on the Supreme Court; the White House would like to include Sotomayor's name as a potential candidate for the open bench slot of associate justice. There would next be an intensive background check. Under no circumstances was Sotomayor to say anything to anyone.[2]

With the election of Senator Barack Obama to the Oval Office in November 2008, the United States was in the throes of some dramatic political changes. Obama, elected as the nation's first African American president, was known as a moderate-to-left politician. Upon his election to the White House, Obama was facing a Congress with a Democratic majority in both houses and a right-leaning Supreme Court, which consisted of four conservatives, four liberals, and a justice who tended to vote toward the right.

Washington insiders predicted that Obama had the opportunity to significantly change the makeup of the court while in office, predicting that the president would get at least one pick, but as many as three or four over the course of his administration. The question was, short of a justice dying while in office, who would retire from the court first? At the time of his election, there appeared to be no one who was thinking of stepping down. But Obama was already thinking ahead about what kind of person would best fit on the current court. In an October 15, 2008, presidential debate, Obama stated that he would "look for those judges who have an outstanding judicial record, who have the intellect, and who hopefully have a sense of what real-world folks are going through."[3]

Obama had a tough road ahead. There were already a number of federal judgeships that needed to be filled and federal judges had already requested of the White House an additional 63 slots be created to fill the increasing caseload of the federal bench. One of the president's legal advisors told CNN that "The [Obama] White House and the Justice Department certainly have people there already thinking about the issues, compiling lists, starting to vet the backgrounds of those candidates." Added to that, the possibility of an empty associate justice seat and the president would have to tread very carefully to make sure his nominees were appointed.[4]

Part of the challenge facing the president was the incredibly high political and practical stakes. Fights over judicial nominees had grown increasingly bitter and were often drawn along party lines. The failed nomination attempt of Robert Bork still hung heavy over the Republicans' heads as did the nasty confirmation proceedings that took place with Clarence Thomas. Many of former President George W. Bush's judicial choices were blocked by Democratic senators, and now, conservative Republicans had promised that President Obama could expect to face challenges over his picks.[5]

According to the White House, President Obama was not interested in provoking a political battle, nor was he going to choose extreme liberal candidates to the federal bench. As one advisor stated, "I don't expect to see President Obama naming some real firebrands, the kind that might be real lightning rods for controversial confirmation hearings. . . . Conservatives are assuming that in his heart of hearts, Obama is a activist, old-fashioned, liberal firebrand on judicial issues, and, at least if one goes by what President Obama has written on the subject, he's not."[6]

Republicans also went a step further by warning the White House that they would not be shut out of the selection process. As one online article noted, "In a March 2 [2009] letter, 41 GOP senators urged Obama 'to consult with us as [he] considers possible nominations to the federal courts from our states.' If not consulted, they said, 'The Republican Conference will be unable to support moving forward on that nominee.' Translation, say liberal groups: filibusters and obstructionist tactics." Even before he started, President Obama was faced with a large headache of a process. Then, not more than two months later, on May 1, 2009, Supreme Court Justice David Souter announced his desire to step down from the bench.[7]

LAYING THE GROUNDWORK

Although Sonia Sotomayor was nowhere to be found on potential candidates lists among the Latino leadership in 1997, things were very different by 2009, when Latino leaders began aggressively laying the groundwork for a potential Sotomayor Supreme Court nomination almost as soon as President Obama was elected. Where Latino groups failed to come together around one candidate during the administrations of George H. W. Bush and Bill Clinton, this time Latino groups were determined to use their influence to get something done. And so began a very systematic courtship between the powerful Latino leaders, Sonia Sotomayor, and the White House.[8]

Things got underway beginning in January 2009 with the appointment of Nydia Velázquez, the Democratic congresswoman from New York's Twelfth District, as the head of the Congressional Hispanic Caucus. Administering Velázquez's oath of office in Washington, D.C., was her longtime friend Sonia Sotomayor who came from New York City for the event. While there, Sotomayor was introduced to every Hispanic member of Congress. Then in May, while attending a Cinco de Mayo party, the White House, Velázquez and another congressman, representing the Bronx, Jose Serrano, made a point of speaking with the president about Sotomayor and the possibility of her as a Supreme Court nominee. Serrano is said to have told President Obama that Sotomayor was not only qualified, but if confirmed, her place on the court bench would have historical import as well. Her appointment to the Supreme Court would also offer the president the opportunity to shape the makeup of the Supreme Court for many years.[9]

After Justice Souter announced his resignation, the Hispanic Caucus met to choose a formal candidate. The meeting was long and litigious, with members siding along ethnic lines. The Mexican Americans wanted a different candidate and were also the majority of members. The Puerto Rican members of the caucus had the candidate but did not have the numbers needed to support Sotomayor without help from other members. Finally, after hours of debating and arguing, Ed Pastor, a Mexican American congressman from Arizona, made a motion to support Sotomayor as a candidate. The group agreed and the meeting ended with a unanimous vote for Sotomayor.[10]

After the Congressional Hispanic Caucus meeting, Velázquez debated as to whether the results of the voting needed to be publicized. There were some concerns on the part of caucus members that if nothing was said before the president announced his picks that the Hispanic community might feel that the caucus had done nothing in the way of putting forth viable Hispanic candidates. In mid-May, she ran into Senator Charles Schumer, of New York, a member of the Judiciary Committee, who told her that he thought it was possible that Sotomayor could be a serious contender for the nomination, but in order for that to happen, the caucus needed to maintain a low profile.[11]

The next step for Latino leaders was to work with African American politicians to secure their support for Sotomayor as well. According to Velázquez, interviewed in a profile piece on Sotomayor for the *New Yorker*, there was a great deal of concern over the potential political fallout that might come in the wake of Obama's nominating a Hispanic to the Supreme Court instead of an African American candidate. For many African Americans, the presence of Clarence Thomas was not enough in terms of feeling represented on the court's bench. It was also clear that Thomas did not have the political cachet among members of the black community like former justice Thurgood Marshall. To that end, Velázquez approached North Carolina representative Mel Watt, a member of the House Judiciary Committee, and who, at one time, served as chair of the Congressional Black Caucus, about the possibility of black congressional members giving their support to Sotomayor. After a few days, Watt contacted Velázquez telling her that he had called the White House and told the president that if there was no suitable African American candidate on the president's short list of nominees, the Black Caucus would throw their support to Sotomayor.[12]

MEET THE CANDIDATE

In the meantime, President Obama was looking over his own list of potential nominees that had been narrowed down to four women:

Diane Wood, of the Seventh Circuit Court of Appeals; Elena Kagan, the Solicitor General; the Homeland Security Secretary, Janet Napolitano; and Sotomayor, who was the only candidate that the president did not know personally. Privately, many on Capitol Hill believed that might disqualify Sotomayor from further consideration by the president.

But unknown to many, Sotomayor was already undergoing an extensive background check as well as interviews with her physician about her diabetes and general health. She also had two extensive interviews with the White House. The first, on April 27, 2009, four days before Justice Souter stated his plans to retire, took place in her New York office with Leslie Kiernan, a partner in the law office of Zuckerman Spaeder. Two days later, Sotomayor was interviewed by phone by Chief of Staff Ron Klain, Cynthia Hogan, who served as Vice President Joe Biden's Counsel, White House Counsel Gregory Craig, and Senior Advisor to the President David Axelrod. Another interview followed with the same people and the Associate Counsel to the President Susan Davies and Chief of Staff Rahm Emanuel.[13]

On the morning of Thursday, May 21, Sotomayor, carrying her customary brown-bag lunch, left her Manhattan condo and strolled past the media cameras that had been watching her. She turned the corner and headed for her office where she met her best friend's husband who drove Sotomayor to Washington. They arrived at the White House around 1:00 P.M. and were taken inside. For the next seven hours, Sotomayor met with Cynthia Hogan, Rahm Emanuel, vetting lawyers, and political strategist David Axelrod who wanted to see how Sotomayor would present herself to the American people as well as the Senate. Finally, Sotomayor met with the president for about an hour. Obama very likely was interested in Sotomayor's personal story, as well as talking to her about the law. Nobody knows for sure because Obama and Sotomayor were the only two people in the room. Clearly though, it was a historic moment with the first African American president talking with possibly the nation's first Hispanic Supreme Court justice. At the end of their meeting, the odds seemed overwhelmingly in Sotomayor's favor. Still Obama told his aides he was taking the weekend to mull over his decision at Camp David.[14]

Sotomayor then left to return to New York City. Later, Vice President Biden called Sotomayor, and the two talked for more than an hour. Sotomayor then talked to her mother and brother telling them that they should be on standby for a trip to Washington in case she was chosen. Later, describing her conversation with the president, Sotomayor said, "It was a conversation like none other that I have ever had."[15]

On Monday, at 8 P.M., Obama told his staff of his choice. At 8:10 P.M., he placed a call to Sotomayor. As she listened to the president, she walked over to the balcony doors of her bedroom with the phone in her right hand as she held her left hand over her chest to try and calm the pounding of her heart. As Sotomayor later described the call:

> And the president got on the phone and said to me, 'Judge, I would like to announce you as my selection to be the next Associate Justice of the United States Supreme Court, . . . And I said to him—I caught my breath and started to cry and said, 'Thank you Mr. President, ... He then asked me to make him two promises. . . . The first was to remain the person I was, and the second was to stay connected to my community. And I said to him that those were two easy promises to make, because those things I could not change.[16]

President Obama then placed calls to the other nominees to let them know he had made his decision.

In New York, Sotomayor began drafting her remarks for the next morning when the announcement would be made. After completing them, she emailed the text and went home to pack. She repeated her earlier subterfuge of appearing to go to work only to slip into her friend's husband's car for the trip to Washington. Sotomayor arrived in Washington at 2:15 A.M. and checked into one of the city's big hotels. With only three hours of sleep, Sotomayor awakened, went through her speech, and got ready to go to the White House. By 7:30 A.M., the unmarked private car arrived for the big event. Sotomayor's family had flown in earlier to be present at the press conference.[17]

On Monday, May 26, President Obama met with members of the press and stated:

President Barack Obama applauds Sonia Sotomayor during a White House East Room ceremony in Washington to announce her nomination on May 26, 2009. (AP Photo/Alex Brandon, FILE)

I've sought the advice of members of Congress on both sides of the aisle, including every member of the Senate Judiciary Committee. My team has reached out to constitutional schol-ars, advocacy organizations and bar associations representing an array of interests and opinions. And I want to thank members of my staff and the administration who have worked so hard and given so much of their time as part of this effort. After completing this exhaustive process, I've decided to nominate an inspiring woman who I believe will make a great justice, Judge Sonia Sotomayor of the great state of New York . . . I hope the Senate acts in a bipartisan fashion, as it has in confirming Judge Sotomayor twice before, and as swiftly as possible, so that she can take her seat on the court in September and participate in deliberations as the court chooses which cases it will hear this coming year.[18]

The president then stepped aside for Sotomayor to address the media gathered there. It appeared that all had gone well with the announcement except for one thing: the White House aides had scrambled the pages of Sotomayor's remarks in the book they placed on the lectern for her. It did not matter. She had memorized her speech.[19]

DETRACTORS

Despite Obama's glowing tribute of Sotomayor and the presence of her mother Celina, seen dabbing at her eyes during the press conference, the introduction of Sonia Sotomayor as Supreme Court nominee got off to a somewhat rough start. Conservatives were already lining up to take their first shots at the new candidate, a situation that President Obama had hoped to avoid.

The initial campaign calling into question Sotomayor's capabilities had begun earlier in the month with the publication of an article in the noted conservative periodical the *New Republic*. The author, Jeffrey Rosen, in his article, "The Case Against Sotomayor," had presented a detailed analysis of why she was an unsuitable candidate. Quoting an anonymous source, Rosen described the prospective nominee:

> Despite the praise from some of her former clerks, and warm words from some of her Second Circuit colleagues, there are also many reservations about Sotomayor. Over the past few weeks, I've been talking to a range of people who have worked with her, nearly all of them former law clerks for other judges on the Second Circuit or former federal prosecutors in New York. Most are Democrats and all of them want President Obama to appoint a judicial star of the highest intellectual caliber who has the potential to change the direction of the court. Nearly all of them acknowledged that Sotomayor is a presumptive front-runner, but nearly none of them raved about her. They expressed questions about her temperament, her judicial craftsmanship, and most of all, her ability to provide an intellectual counterweight to the conservative justices, as well as a clear liberal alternative.

The most consistent concern was that Sotomayor, although an able lawyer, was "not that smart and kind of a bully on the bench," as one former Second Circuit clerk for another judge put it. "She has an inflated opinion of herself, and is domineering during oral arguments, but her questions aren't penetrating and don't get to the heart of the issue." (During one argument, an elderly judicial colleague is said to have leaned over and said, "Will you please stop talking and let them talk?")[20]

Within hours of the piece's posting on its website, there were already a number of comments; in all, the article generated 642 responses, many of them taking Rosen to task for his brutal portrait of Sotomayor. Rosen would eventually back down in some of his criticisms, and he softened others, but other media outlets and writers began chiming in with their own take on Sotomayor's nomination.

On May 27, the day after the president announced Sotomayor's nomination, journalist Dana Milbank wrote in the Washington *Post* that Obama had opted for "biography over brain." Former Speaker of the House and noted Republican conservative Newt Gingrich made use of social media, using Twitter to call Sotomayor a "Latina woman racist." The idea posited by conservatives and supporters of the other candidates painted a picture of Sotomayor as temperamental and as one reporter noted an "intellectually invalid candidate" making what promised to be a rocky road to the nomination hearings even more so.[21]

Richard Epstein while writing about the nomination in *Forbes* magazine took both the president and the nominee to task:

> Evidently, the characteristics that matter most for a potential nominee to the Supreme Court have little to do with judicial ability or temperament, or even so ephemeral a consideration as a knowledge of the law. Instead, the tag line for this appointment says it all. The president wants to choose "a daughter of Puerto Rican parents raised in Bronx public housing projects to become the nation's first Hispanic justice." Obviously, none of these factors disqualifies anyone for the Supreme Court. But affirmative action standards are a bad way to pick one of the nine

most influential jurists in the U.S., whose vast powers can shape virtually every aspect of our current lives.[22]

32 WORDS

In addition to the unflattering comments and editorials that were appearing in the national periodicals and newspapers about Sotomayor, political conservatives were also honing in on a speech that Sotomayor made in 2001. The talk that was presented as the Judge Mario G. Olmos Memorial Lecture was delivered to an audience at the University of California, Berkeley, School of Law. In her speech, Sotomayor spoke about the underrepresentation of women and Hispanics in the legal profession. She stated that when speaking about legal decisions made in the areas of race and sexual discrimination, that even though the attorneys who argued these historic decisions before the Supreme Court were often African Americans or women, the majority of decisions have been made by older, white men. She then stated:

> Whether born from experience or inherent physiological or cultural differences . . . our gender and national origins may and will make a difference in our judging. Justice [Sandra] O'Connor has often been cited as saying that a wise old man and wise old woman will reach the same conclusion in deciding cases. . . . I am also not so sure that I agree with the statement. First, as Professor Martha Minnow has noted, there can never be a universal definition of wise. Second, I would hope that a wise Latina woman with the richness of her experiences would more often than not reach a better conclusion than a white male who hasn't lived that life.[23]

The "32 words" as they were called, unleashed another torrent of criticism from Sotomayor opponents. Rush Limbaugh described Sotomayor as "reverse racist." The conservative Judicial Confirmation Network accused her of a "personal political agenda" and that her nomination should be blocked. Conservative advocacy groups argued that the Sotomayor nomination could force an "emotional battle" over the tricky issues of race and affirmative action.[24]

The White House moved quickly to stop any more potential damage to the Sotomayor nomination. White House Press Secretary Robert Gibbs, in his weekly briefing, pointed out that Sotomayor's remarks were taken out of context and stated, "Look at the totality of it. I have confidence that people will come to a reasonable conclusion." Gibbs also stated that when the president was deciding on the qualities he was looking for in a potential nominee, "a diverse background was atop the list." The press secretary also said that when talks about "the richness of experience, I include a life and an upbringing that are different than some people have had."[25]

A column written by Carolina A. Miranda for *Time* magazine asked what the fuss was all about. For Miranda, a Latina writer and journalist, Sotomayor's comments simply were trying to convey the importance of taking into account other people's cultural experiences, or "that her [Sotomayor's] breadth of experience navigating different worlds might lead her to have greater wisdom on certain topics than her white male counterparts." Miranda also looked to a white male to bolster her argument: "It is no different from what [Justice] Samuel Alito said in 2006 ('when I get a case about discrimination, I have to think about people in my own family who suffered discrimination because of their ethnic background or because of religion or because of gender'.) Our varied experiences shape us, they enrich us, they give us the ability to . . . empathize."[26]

SUPPORTERS

Even as conservative GOP members were pointing out the problems with Sotomayor's nomination, there was also a growing chorus of support. Many pointed out that the unflattering portrayal of Sotomayor as a judge demonstrated a profound misreading of how courtrooms, especially at the federal level operate. In the case of the Second Circuit, time is of the essence as lawyers have roughly 10 minutes to present their arguments, which means comments need to be brief and even curt. Further, Sotomayor's supporters were as quick to point out as conservatives were quick to tar her with the brush of racism that the conservative characterization of Sotomayor drew on common stereotypes of "the dense lady-judge, the mouthy Latina." Judge Guido Calabresi, who taught Sotomayor at Yale, in speaking to the *New York Times* called the charges sexist. In June, Ted Shaw, a former head of the NAACP Legal and Educational Defense Fund, and a high-school classmate of Sotomayor's, told a writer for the *New Yorker*, that Sotomayor "was at the top of our class, which was ninety percent white. For those who suggest her intellectual background is not strong—well, all the white folks were below her!"[27]

In an attempt to quell the criticisms, the Obama Administration also called on outside validators, which included her former boss Robert Morgenthau, Vice President Joe Biden, and the chief of Miami police, John Timoney, who told Sotomayor that law-enforcement officials were supporting her. Hugh H. Mo, who had supervised Sotomayor in the DA's office, wrote an article for *Politico*, detailing Sotomayor's role in helping to convict the Tarzan burglar. The White House also brought on board Louis Freeh, the FBI director under Bill Clinton and, for a short time also under George W. Bush and who had served with Sotomayor as a district-court judge. Freeh's job was to assure Republican lawyers that in supporting Sotomayor they would not be hurting themselves politically.[28]

The strategy worked. As the *New Yorker* profile piece pointed out that Conservatives, stymied by Sotomayor's credentials and backing were left criticizing typing mistakes such as misspelled proper names or subject-verb agreement. The Republican senators who would be called upon to vote on the nomination also remained relatively quiet. Other Republicans trod cautiously in stating their opposition to the first Hispanic Supreme Court nominee.[29]

Even some of Sotomayor's supporters were holding their breath. Congressman Jose Serrano later said of the early days after Sotomayor's nomination was announced, that "I was concerned at the beginning, when I saw the onslaught of the right-wing radio stations and TV shows, but then I realized it wasn't universal." Serrano also realized that given the large number of white men that Sotomayor had worked with, and who had come out in support of her nomination, that in the end, everything would work out just fine."[30]

STEPPING CAREFULLY

No matter what they thought privately, many Republican Party strategists as well as politicians saw the need to move warily and carefully around the Sotomayor nomination. GOP party strategists told Republican senators that to attack Sotomayor also meant chasing away and alienating potential Hispanic voters, many of whom tended to vote along conservative lines. The Republicans had also noted that in recent years, many Hispanic voters had turned their backs on the party because of conservative stances on issues such as support for tough immigration restrictions and the opposition of legalizing undocumented workers. Robert de Posada, who worked as a GOP strategist stated that given that the Republican Party was concerned about reaching Latino voters in the future, it was not in their best interest to oppose Sotomayor's nomination too strenuously or viciously.[31]

Lionel Sosa, a Texas-based Republican ad maker who designed Latino outreach for Republican presidents Ronald Reagan, George Bush, and George W. Bush, described that by opposing Sotomayor, the Republicans would essentially be running the risk of antagonizing Latino voters, who, have in the past often thrown their support toward conservative candidates. To go up against Sotomayor would be courting disaster politically from one of the nation's fastest growing minorities. Congressional Republicans took the warnings seriously and during the weeks leading to the nomination hearings, conferred with Latino party strategists over how best to mount an opposition that was not deemed mean spirited or partisan, particularly by a political party that is dominated by Southern, conservative white men.[32]

THE COURTESY CALLS

While her supporters and detractors were making their cases before the American public, Sotomayor had other things on her mind. Before her confirmation hearings were set to begin on July 13, Sotomayor paid courtesy calls to 89 senators over a two-week period. Her visits were the most that any Supreme Court nominee has ever undertaken. It was Sotomayor's hope that by meeting the senators she might have an opportunity to speak with those men and women who would eventually be called upon to vote on her nomination. Sotomayor also hoped to present her side of the controversial remarks about her judicial demeanor and where she stands on particular issues such as abortion rights. She also wanted to show her personal side in talking about the Yankees, or joking about the cast on her ankle, which she had fractured at LaGuardia Airport when she tripped on a ramp.[33]

When Sotomayor met with Senator Amy Klobuchar of Minnesota, the senator said, "I had read news accounts of these anonymous comments, so I thought, What's she going to be like? . . . It turned out she was incredibly engaging. She was ten minutes early and we ran into each other in the hallway. Most people would be, like, 'O.K., we're meeting in ten minutes,' but she looked at me, and she goes, 'I'm here already,' and I said, 'Well, do you want to come in?'" When Sotomayor met with Senator Lindsey Graham of South Carolina, Graham questioned her about reports made anonymously about Sotomayor's conduct on the bench. Said Graham, "I said it was a concern to me, I don't like bully judges. She said, 'I sure am not.'"[34]

While visiting with Cuban-born Senator Mel Martinez, the senator from Florida, the two spoke Spanish. Her conversation with Illinois Senator Dick Durbin centered about the early deaths of both their fathers. In speaking with Democratic senators who received advice about how to handle her critics, Chuck Schumer, the Democratic senator from New York remembers telling Sotomayor that the "the most important thing is to be yourself because she's such a powerful presence and such a powerful person . . . When you meet her person to person, sitting across a table a couple of inches apart, her personality—you know, it's shining, it's strong, comes through."[35]

But not everyone was taken with the judge from New York City. Senator Jim DeMint, a South Carolina Republican, became irked when Sotomayor refused to take a firm stand on gun rights or the question of whether an unborn child has rights. He later said that Sotomayor claimed that she had never thought about those issues in those terms. In meeting with Senator David Vitter from Louisiana, she found the senator most unwelcoming. As Sotomayor later told a friend, Vitter said to her, "I want to ask you—do you think if I was you, and I had made the wise-Latina comment that you made, that I would have deserved to be a Supreme Court Justice?," to which Sotomayor replied, "If you had my record, yes."[36]

Finally, the meetings were at an end. By July 12, Sotomayor had done all she could do. On July 13, she along with the American viewing public would be seated and ready to begin the next phase of the process: her confirmation hearings.

NOTES

1. Deborah Tedford, "Obama Chooses Sotomayor for High Court," *NPR*, May 26, 2009, http://www.npr.org/templates/story/story.php?storyId=104530389.

2. Antonia Felix, *Sonia Sotomayor: The True American Dream*, New York: Berkeley Publishing Group, 2010, p. 209.

3. Bill Mears, "Analysis: Obama's First Judicial Pick Signals Fight for Control," *CNNPolitics*, March 18, 2009, http://articles.cnn.com/2009–03–18/politics/obama.judiciary_1_judicial-choices-su preme-court-obama-white-house?_s=PM:POLITICS.

4. Ibid.

5. Ibid.

6. Ibid.

7. Ibid.

8. Lauren Collins, "Number Nine: Sonia Sotomayor's High Profile Debut," *New Yorker*, January 11, 2010, p. 48.

9. Ibid.

10. Ibid.

11. Ibid.

12. Ibid.

13. "Senate Questionnaire Details Sotomayor's Interviews," *The BLT: The Blog of LegalTimes*, June 4, 2009, http://legaltimes.typepad.com/blt/2009/06/sotomayor-submits-questionnaire-to-senate-judiciary.html.

14. Bill Mears, "Analysis: Obama's First Judicial Pick Signals Fight for Control," *CNNPolitics*, March 18, 2009, http://www.cnn.com/2009/POLITICS/03/18/obama.judiciary/index.html?iref=allsearch.

15. Ilana Seagar, "Sotomayor Law '79 Returns to Speak at Law School Reunion," *Yale Daily News*, October 19, 2009, http://www.yaledailynews.com/news/2009/oct/19/sotomayor-law-79-returns-to-speak-at-law-school/.

16. Joan Biskupic, "Sotomayor Says Obama's Job Offer Set Her Heart Racing," *USA Today*, September 25, 2009, http://www.usatoday.com/news/washington/judicial/2009–09–24-sotomayor_N.htm.

17. Felix, *Sonia Sotomayor*, p. 216.

18. "Obama's Sotomayor Nomination Remarks," *MSNBC White House*, May 26, 2009, http://www.msnbc.msn.com/id/30943237/ns/politics-white_house/t/obamas-sotomayor-nomination-remarks/#.TptFrZtKO5I.

19. Nina Totenberg, "How Obama's Nomination of Sotomayor Unfolded," *NPR*, May 28, 2009, http://www.npr.org/templates/story/story.php?storyId=104648062.

20. Jeffrey Rosen, "The Case Against Sotomayor," *The New Republic*, May 4, 2009, http://www.tnr.com/article/politics/the-case-against-sotomayor.

21. Collins, "Number Nine: Sonia Sotomayor's High Profile Debut."

22. Richard A. Epstein, "The Sotomayor Nomination," *Forbes*, May 26, 2009, http://www.forbes.com/2009/05/26/supreme-court-nomination-obama-opinions-columnists-sonia-sotomayor.html.

23. Sonia Sotomayor, "Lecture: A Latina Judge's Voice," *New York Times*, May 14, 2009, http://www.nytimes.com/2009/05/15/us/politics/15judge.text.html?pagewanted=1.

24. Peter Wallstein and Richard Simon, "Sotomayor Nomination Splits GOP," *Los Angeles Times*, May 27, 2009, http://articles.latimes.com/2009/may/27/nation/na-court-assess27.

25. "'Latina Woman' Remark may Dominate Hearings," *CNNPolitics*, Mary 28, 2009, http://articles.cnn.com/2009–05–28/politics/sotomayor.latina.remark.reax_1_latina-white-house-supreme-court?_s=PM:POLITICS.

26. Carolina A. Miranda, "Just What is a 'Wise Latina' Anyway?," *Time*, July 14, 2009, http://www.time.com/time/politics/article/0,8599,1910403,00.html.

27. Collins, "Number Nine: Sonia Sotomayor's High Profile Debut."

28. Ibid.

29. Ibid.

30. Ibid.

31. Ibid.

32. Ibid.

33. Robert Barnes, "Left and Right Begin Battle Over Sotomayor's Supreme Court Nomination," *Washington Post*, May 28, 2009, http://www.washingtonpost.com/wp-dyn/content/article/2009/05/27/AR2009052703713.html?sid=ST2009052703896; Joan Biskupic, "Sotomayor Courtesy Calls, Not Photo Ops," *USA Today*, June 18, 2009, http://www.usatoday.com/news/washington/judicial/2009–06–18-sotomayor-senate_N.htm.

34. Ibid.

35. "Senators say Sotomayor Impressive in Meetings," *USA Today*, June 14, 2009, http://www.usatoday.com/news/washington/2009–06–13-sotomayor-interviews_N.htm.

36. Collins, "Number Nine: Sonia Sotomayor's High Profile Debut," p. 49.

Chapter 10

JUSTICE SOTOMAYOR

In the past month, many senators have asked me about my judicial philosophy. . . . It is simple: fidelity to the law. The task of a judge is not to make law, it is to apply the law. And it is clear, I believe, that my record . . . reflects my rigorous commitment to interpreting the Constitution according to its terms, interpreting statutes according to their terms and Congress's intent and hewing faithfully to precedents established by the Supreme Court and by my Circuit Court. In each case I have heard, I have applied the law to the facts at hand.

I am here today because of her aspirations and sacrifices. Mom, I love that we are sharing this together.[1]

—Sonia Sotomayor, speaking at her confirmation hearings,
July 13, 2009

PARTY POLITICS

It appeared that nothing about the Sonia Sotomayor nomination was going to go easily. As soon as Senate Democrats announced that they would move as quickly as possible to have Sotomayor appointed and that her hearings would begin in mid-July, a storm of Republican protests was unleashed. Senator Patrick Leahy from Vermont, who served as the Senate Judiciary Committee chairman and also a Democrat, announced that he would convene the hearings on July 13. He also stated that the date, roughly two months after President Obama's nomination of Sotomayor, presented a "fair and adequate" schedule that was comparable to other Supreme Court nominees. The timing too took into consideration the late-summer break that takes place in Congress every August. The Republican leader of the Senate, Mitch McConnell of Kentucky, immediately called Leahy's tactics "heavy-handed," and asked the Democrats to reconsider scheduling the hearings. In an article for the Associated Press, McConnell stated, "Let me be clear. . . . Because of what our Democratic colleagues are doing and the way they are doing it, it will now be much more difficult to achieve the kind of comity and cooperation on this and other matters that we need and expect around here." Republicans also stated that they needed more time to review Sotomayor's record and that a September vote would be more reasonable, while also allowing enough time for Sotomayor, if she was appointed to take the bench by the beginning of the October session.[2]

Leahy stated again that there was no reason to delay Sotomayor's hearings and that she deserved the opportunity to address criticisms and questions about her record as soon as possible. Leahy also reminded the Republican senators that "This is a historic nomination, and I hope all senators will cooperate. . . . She deserves a fair hearing—not trial by attack and assaults about her character." However, the Republicans also knew that Leahy had them over a barrel: to make a fuss over the timetable would cause further problems of perceptions by the public that the GOP was simply trying to hold up the nomination because of party differences. They also realized that they needed to be very careful in going up against Sotomayor, who if appointed, would be the first Hispanic on the Supreme Court of the United States.[3]

Instead, the Republicans complained about the schedule. They also warned they were planning to play tough at the hearings. Said Senator Jeff Sessions of Alabama, who emerged as one of Sotomayor's more vocal critics, "I'm going to insist that we do it right . . . This rush is ill-advised." As a part of their argument, Republicans pointed out that a little over three months had elapsed between the nomination of Justice Samuel Alito and his confirmation. They also reminded their critics that Sotomayor had made over 3,000 rulings, which suggested that more time was needed in order to study her cases and outcomes.[4]

HEARINGS

On a Monday morning, July 13, 2009, Sonia Sotomayor, dressed in a cobalt blue suit, her fingernails wearing a neutral shade of polish (all of Sotomayor's wardrobe choices were stipulated by the White House), was seated at a long wooden table, listening to the opening statements of the 19 members of the Senate Judiciary Committee. Seated on either side of her were New York Democratic senators Chuck Schumer and Kirsten Gillibrand. On the table was a microphone and two plastic glasses with water. Her fractured ankle was resting on a makeshift footrest that had been rigged with duct tape.[5]

Sonia Sotomayor returns to Capitol Hill in Washington, D.C., after a break in her confirmation hearing before the Senate Judiciary Committee, July 13, 2009. (AP Photo/Ron Edmonds)

Sotomayor's head, no doubt, was filled with all kinds of thoughts, including some helpful hints passed on by Tom Korologos, a former United States ambassador to Belgium. Korologos had made a second career of advising presidential nominees on how to behave in front of committees such as this. In a piece done for the *Washington Post*, Korologos offered a number of practical tips:

> Hearings can be judged by the 80–20 rule. If the senators are speaking 80 percent of the time, you're doing fine. If it's 60–40, you are arguing with them. If it's 50–50, you've blown it . . . You are not required to defend your predecessor or his job performance. Neither are you permitted to dump on him. Remember, you know more about the subject than they do. But don't embarrass them. "I don't know" is an acceptable answer. "Let me provide the answer for the record later on" is much better than guessing.
>
> Do not give away the store to get confirmed. Stick with the president's policy positions.
>
> Instruct those attending with you that no one is allowed to pass notes to you while you are in the chair. You sit alone because you don't need help from others. If you make a mistake, the staff will let you know during a break, and you can correct it during the next round of questioning. If a senator makes a policy suggestion, do not endorse it. Instead, say: "Senator, that is an excellent and interesting concept I would like to examine—if confirmed." If you get a particularly tough or esoteric question, go with your instincts. But notice also that a pitcher of water is provided. If you get a contentious question, pour a glass of water. It will give you an additional 10 seconds to think of a good answer.[6]

Sotomayor had also undergone weeks of what were known as "murder boards," during which White House staff quizzed her on the latest legal developments. Sotomayor showed that she was current on business law but was less familiar with administrative legal developments. She was also coached on how to handle the senators. For instance, she was never to interrupt while a senator was speaking, as he was speaking not just to the gallery of attendants but also to television. At the end of each day, she returned to her suite at the Crowne Plaza Hotel, where surrounded by binders of information she would wolf down cereal for her dinner and then go to bed. Also adding to the stress was the inconvenience of her fractured ankle, which meant that her courtesy calls to various senators had to be conducted from the office of Senator Dick Durbin where she could rest in a chair and meet with various people.[7]

UNDERWAY

The opening volley from the Republicans came in less than 22 minutes into the hearing. Senator Jeff Sessions stated, "I think it is noteworthy that, when asked about Judge Sotomayor's now famous statement that a 'wise Latina' would come to a better conclusion than others, President Obama, White House Press Secretary Robert Gibbs, and Supreme Court Justice Ginsburg declined to defend the substance of those remarks." A writer for the *New Yorker* magazine described the next few moments: "Sotomayor regarded the senators with withering impassivity. When Senator Lindsey Graham, of South Carolina, who emerged as Sotomayor's most eloquent and provocative antagonist, delivered one of the hearing's most memorable lines—'If I had said anything remotely like that, my career would have been over'—she looked as though she had smelled something bad."[8]

Sotomayor was given the opportunity to make some remarks of her own in which she addressed some of the concerns posed by the committee. She told the committee that she swore "fidelity to the law" and "rigorous commitment" to the Constitution as guiding her judicial philosophy. Sotomayor also stated that while in the courtroom, neither ethnicity, gender, or empathy played a role in her decisions. She also promised to serve in the "larger interest of impartial justice." Still, it was clear that lines had been drawn and the next two days would not be easy ones for the nominee. Adding to the atmosphere in the room, were the periodic outbursts of several antiabortion protesters who at points interrupted the committee's opening statements.[9]

DAYS 2 AND 3

On Tuesday, the second day of the hearings, Sotomayor had more of an opportunity to answer questions. Judiciary committee Chairman

Senator Patrick Leahy got things underway when he asked Sotomayor several questions on the role of a judge. Sotomayor replied that in judging what was key to the process was "keeping an open mind. It's the process of not coming to a decision with a prejudgment ever of an outcome." She also told the committee that judges must make decisions that are "limited to what the law says on the facts before the judge." Sotomayor's response was also intended to head off growing Republican concerns that she would rely too much on empathy if she were confirmed. Senator Jeff Sessions grudgingly admitted that Sotomayor was hitting the right notes but that "had you been saying that with clarity over the last decade or 15 years, we'd have a lot fewer problems today."[10]

Sotomayor also took time to take issue with a statement made by President Obama when he was a senator in 2005. According to the president, in a certain number of judicial decisions, "the critical ingredient is supplied by what is in the judge's heart." Arizona Republican Senator Jon Kyl asked Sotomayor whether she agreed with the president's statement. Sotomayor's response: "No, sir, I wouldn't approach the issue of judging the way the president does." She added, "I can only explain what I think judges should do. . . . Judges can't rely on what's in their heart. . . . It's not the heart that compels conclusions in cases, it's the law."[11]

Sotomayor also stated that judges need to make their decisions for each case based on specific facts and specific laws, rather than on empathy or personal considerations. She defended her judicial record as free from personal or ethnic bias. Sotomayor also emphasized the importance of recognizing the Supreme Court's present positions on such hot button issues as abortion, gun rights, and affirmative action.[12]

Senator Sessions then told Sotomayor that he was troubled by a number of her rulings and in effect suggested that contrary to what she had said about being free of bias, that her background would play a role in deciding cases. Sotomayor rejected outright Session's inferences and stated, that "My record shows that at no point in time have I permitted my personal views or sympathies to influence the outcome of a case. . . . In every case where I have identified a sympathy, I have articulated it and explained to the litigant why the law requires a different result."[13]

THE "WISE LATINA" REVISITED

Even as her supporters took every opportunity to again emphasize Sotomayor's public record, her detractors focused more on statements made by Sotomayor while not sitting on the bench. One of these was the infamous "Wise Latina" remarks made by Sotomayor in 2001. Committee Chairman Patrick Leahy said her critics had twisted her meaning in that speech and looking at Sotomayor told her it was time to answer her critics on the record. "Here's your chance," he said. "You tell us what's going on here, judge," to which Sotomayor replied, "Thank you for giving me an opportunity to explain my remark."[14]

In her remarks to the committee about the phrase and its meaning Sotomayor stated, "The context of the words that I spoke have created a misunderstanding," adding that the term was one that she has often used to groups of women lawyers or to Latino groups and that she was "trying to inspire them to believe that their life experience would enrich the legal system." Sotomayor also went on to say that, "To give everyone assurances, I want to state upfront, unequivocally and without doubt, I do not believe that any ethnic, racial or gender group has an advantage in sound judging. I do believe that every person has equal opportunity to become a good and wise judge, regardless of their background or life experiences." With some understatement, Sonia Sotomayor told the Judiciary Committee that "no words I have ever spoken received so much attention."[15]

Sotomayor went further, saying that she was attempting a play on words used in a famous quote from former Supreme Court Justice Sandra Day O'Connor, who often said that she did not view herself as a female jurist, and that if a wise old man and a wise old woman were judging the same case, they both would reach the same result. But where O'Connor was trying to show that there was no gender bias on the bench, Sotomayor's comment appeared to strike a different response in stating that gender, particularly a woman's opinion as a judge, would often be the wiser choice. "I was trying to play on her words—my play fell flat. That was bad," Sotomayor said. "It left an impression that life experiences commanded a result in cases, but that is not what I do as a judge."

Senator Lindsey Graham of South Carolina was still not going to let Sotomayor off the hook. At one point, Graham stated that if he had made a similar comment like Sotomayor's "wise Latina" during a political race, his opponents "would have my head." He then went on to say to Sotomayor: "It would make national news and it should. Having said that I am not going to judge you by that one statement. I just hope you'll appreciate the world we live in, meaning *you* can say those things and still inspire somebody and still get a chance to get on the Supreme Court. If others used those words, they 'wouldn't survive.'" Graham then asked Sotomayor if his comments made sense to her. She stated it did.[16]

TWO R'S: RICCI AND ROE

Later that day, Sotomayor was asked to address one of the more controversial decisions she made as judge in the case of *Ricci v. DeStefano*. The case had its origins in 2003, with the city of New Haven, Connecticut Fire Department offering written and oral examinations for promotion in the department for the ranks of Lieutenant and Captain. Under the contract between the city and the New Haven firefighters' union, the written exam result would count for 60 percent of an applicant's overall score while the oral exam would count for the remaining 40 percent. A passing grade would be anything above 70 percent.[17]

A total of 188 firefighters took the exam, with the passing rate for African American firefighters approximately half of that for white firefighters. In all, 20 firefighters, 19 white and 1 Hispanic, passed the exam for the promotions. However, the city of New Haven decided to invalidate the test results because no black firefighters had scored high enough to be considered for promotion. In defending their actions, the city stated that it feared a lawsuit over the "test's adverse impact on a protected minority." The firefighters who passed claimed that they were victims of a reverse racial discrimination; they were denied the promotions because they were white.[18]

In 2004, the 20 firefighters took their case to court on those grounds, stating that they would have won their promotions if they had been African American. Among the white firefighters associated with the case was Frank Ricci. Ricci, who was dyslexic, paid extra money to have the test materials converted to an audio format that would help him to take the test. Ricci ended up scoring very well on the exam and, if the city had followed through on its original plan, would have been promoted.[19]

The lawyer for the firefighters, Karen Lee Torte wrote in her brief that "The court has made clear that meaningful equality under the [Constitution's] equal protection clause and equal opportunity under Title VII are not achieved by discriminating against one group of individuals to benefit another group on account of race . . . Petitioners ask nothing more than the basic American right to be judged by who they are and what they have accomplished, not by the color of their skin." An interesting side note to the case was that there was no explanation in the court briefs as to why African American candidates did not score as well on the exam. Instead, the city of New Haven focused on the racial makeup of the pass-fail mix in test scores. City officials also believed that there was some disparity and bias in the test content and format.[20]

The court case wound up in front of the Second Circuit Court where Sotomayor was part of a three-judge panel that ruled against the firefighters. That court threw the case out, stating that taking the test only meant that the firefighters could gain a promotion; that the test did not guarantee a job. The firefighters appealed and the case eventually made its way to the Supreme Court, which disagreed with Sotomayor and overturned the ruling. In the audience that afternoon for the hearings, were some of the firefighters who initially brought the suit, including Frank Ricci and Ben Vargas who offered testimony.[21]

Ricci told the committee that he believed that "Achievement is neither limited nor determined by one's race, but by one's skills, dedication, commitment and character. . . . At some point we began to understand that this case was no longer about the 20 of us, but about so many other Americans who had lost faith in the court system because of what happened to us. We understood that fire fighters and others of all races and different ethnicities wanted what we sought, which was simple fairness, the right to be judged on merit, and the rules and the law to be enforced evenhandedly."[22]

Ben Vargas also spoke in a similar fashion by telling the committee that he "played by the rules, and then endured a long process of asking the court to enforce those rules." But the courts, he added, "didn't care." When he learned of the decision by Sotomayor and the Second

Circuit court, Vargas said, "We were devastated to see a one-paragraph unpublished order summarily dismissing our case, and indeed even the notion that that we had presented important legal issues to that court of appeals." In her defense, Sotomayor said that it was decided "on the basis of a very thorough, 78-page decision by the district court and on the basis of established precedent—not on her opinion of what the preferred outcome of the case should be."[23]

Over the course of the afternoon, Sotomayor was also asked her opinion on several other controversial issues including abortion with the Supreme Court's ruling in the 1973 decision in *Roe v. Wade* and 1992's *Planned Parenthood of Southeastern Pennsylvania v Casey*. In answering the committee, Sotomayor was very careful in stating the precedents that the Supreme Court set, making clear that those rulings defined the current state of abortion laws in the United States. While her critics called her answers nonresponsive, others pointed out that it suggested that Sotomayor would be a judge who made decisions based on the law, not on preconceived opinions whether they were hers or the public's.[24]

The next day, Sotomayor was also asked about her opinion of the Second Amendment's right to bear arms. However, when pressed, she refused to elaborate on her views about firearm regulations by simply stating that she would "make no prejudgments" about future firearms-related cases. Sotomayor also stated that she believed that Americans currently did not enjoy the fundamental right to bear arms, a view that remained consistent with two previous rulings she issued as an appeals court judge. Sotomayor also talked to the committee about the fact that existing decisions of the Supreme Court only limits "the actions the federal government could take with respect to the possession of firearms." This means that the court cannot be used to strike down state laws that may be more broad in their interpretation.

A COMPOSED NOMINEE

In general, those covering the nomination hearings found Sotomayor to be calm, speaking in measured tones, even as some senators raised their voices to her. Her demeanor was such that it seemed to disprove the earlier anonymous claims that her temperament was aggressive or bullying. The nominee's tone in the hearing was consistently slow and measured. She seemed to be striving not to create any drama. At one point, Lindsey Graham asked Sotomayor if she thought she had a temperament problem. "No, sir," replied Sotomayor. "I believe that my reputation is such that I ask the hard questions, but I do it evenly for both sides." California Senator Dianne Feinstein found Sotomayor's behavior circumspect, stating that "This very reserved, very factual and very considered nominee is being characterized as being an activist when she is anything but."[25]

Later during an afternoon break, some senators weighed more on Sotomayor's performance during the hearings. Lindsey Graham said, "She's doing okay . . . [she] was very reasoned and measured and seems to have a good understanding of the law." The Democrats on the committee were more enthusiastic with Chairman Patrick Leahy of Vermont saying that he fully expected Sotomayor to win the support from both parties and that her appointment seemed secure. Sheldon Whitehouse, a Democratic Senator from Rhode Island agreed, saying that "I don't think she showed the least difficulty with her temperament or with her capacity to remember and answer complex questions. . . . I thought it was a bravura performance, both in her intellect and her temperament [which] showed somebody who I could very readily see sitting behind that high bench on the Supreme Court."[26]

Finally, after the final round of questions on Wednesday morning, the afternoon was dedicated to witness testimonies, which included appearances by Robert Morgenthau and the New Haven firefighters Frank Ricci and Ben Vargas. For those who thought Ricci would be the smoking gun, which might be used to derail the hearings and Sotomayor's nomination, they were disappointed. Ricci simply stated that he wanted a chance to tell his side of the story and that he had no opinion to express publicly about her ruling or her nomination.[27]

A number of publications consulted legal experts throughout the country to ask their opinions on the Sotomayor hearings. In general, many were disappointed, even critical of the hearings, the committee and Sotomayor herself, such as the commentary from Peggy Noonan:

Looking at things shallowly, and let's, Sonia Sotomayor seemed weirdly over rehearsed, speaking very slowly, gesturing with her hands in a way that was no doubt supposed to look natural and warm, like grandma in the kitchen, but instead came across as artificial and mildly animatronic.

She took refuge (as did some of her questioners) in the impenetrable language of the law, and in what seemed (and this is becoming a regular strategy in politics) to be the deliberate jumbling of syntax, so people at home won't be able to follow what is being said. To be clear and succinct is to look for trouble. Better to produce a mist and miasma of jumbly words, and sentences that do not hold.[28]

Alan Dershowitz posited that the "confirmation hearings for Supreme Court Justices bring out the worst in the senators and in the nominee. The Sotomayor hearings are worse than most. Senators pretend to be outraged by the thought that a judge might be influenced by ethnicity, gender, religion, political affiliation or other such factors. The nominee pretends that she misspoke, or was misunderstood, when she acknowledged, in a moment of candor, that her Latina background might put her in a better position to understand certain legal or constitutional issues."[29]

Philip K. Howard also found the proceedings disappointing, calling them "almost devoid of substance, so the lessons are mainly negative. The one useful conclusion is that Judge Sotomayor's skill at parrying loaded questions demonstrates that she is as smart as her resume suggests. Otherwise, the hearings are a waste of time. We don't know what Judge Sotomayor really believes, because everything has been scripted to avoid any discussion of substance. The hearings are more about the senators campaigning to the television audience."[30]

CONFIRMED!

The 10-week struggle to have Sonia Sotomayor confirmed finally ended on July 16, when the United States Senate voted to appoint her as the 111th Justice for the United States Supreme Court. The final vote was 68 to 31, as each member rose one by one to cast his or her vote. To no one's surprise, the voting broke down largely along party lines, though nine Republicans cast their votes in favor of the judge from

New York City. One noted Democrat, Senator Edward M. Kennedy of Massachusetts, was ill and so did not cast a vote. One of the more notable voters was Senator Robert C. Byrd, the 91-year-old Democrat of West Virginia. Senator Byrd, who also had been ailing, made a rare appearance in the Senate chambers, coming in his wheelchair. He cast his vote with a smile when his name was called. The vote was historic. Sonia Sotomayor became the first Hispanic to ascend to the nation's highest court.[31]

Sotomayor's confirmation was also a tremendous victory for the Obama administration. Upon hearing that his nominee had won her appointment, the president said that her confirmation was "breaking yet another barrier and moving us yet another step closer to a more perfect union." "With this historic vote," Obama continued, "the Senate has affirmed that Judge Sotomayor has the intellect, the temperament, the history, the integrity and the independence of mind to ably serve on our nation's highest court." Sotomayor was formally confirmed on Saturday at a private ceremony at the Supreme Court building.[32]

Sotomayor, now back in New York City, watched the historic vote unfold from her chambers. After learning of the Senate's decision, she refrained from making any comments or issuing any statements. However, when she arrived at her West Village residence that evening, she smiled and waved to the neighbors who had gathered near her house. When she came home, the audience clapped and shouted her name.[33]

Still some Republicans were not happy with the outcome. Senator Mitch McConnell commented that although "Judge Sotomayor is certainly a fine person with an impressive story and a distinguished background . . . a judge must be able to check his or her personal or political agenda at the courtroom door and do justice evenhandedly, as the judicial oath requires. This is the most fundamental test. It is a test that Judge Sotomayor does not pass." Other Republicans were cautious in their opposition to her nomination, while emphasizing that they were not anti-Hispanic. Before announcing his opposition to her nomination, Senator John McCain of Arizona described her as an "immensely qualified candidate" with an "inspiring and compelling" life story. Still, other Capitol Hill watchers wondered if the Hispanic community would remember the overtures made by Republicans toward them, or if they would choose to recall how the GOP tried to block the nomination of the first Hispanic to the Supreme Court.[34]

JUSTICE SOTOMAYOR

At just past 11 A.M. on Saturday, August 6, 2009, Chief Justice John G. Roberts Jr. administered a pair of oaths in two private ceremonies at the Supreme Court building, confirming Sonia Sotomayor as an Associate Justice to the Supreme Court. During the first ceremony, Chief Justice Roberts, Justice Anthony M. Kennedy, Justice Sotomayor's immediate family that included her mother and brother, Judge Robert Katzmann of the United States Court of Appeals for the Second Circuit, members of the chief justice's staff, and a court photographer were present. Holding the Bible for the ceremony was Sonia's mother.[35]

Wearing a cream-colored suit, but minus the walking cast that she had worn during the confirmation hearings, Sotomayor took the stan-

Sonia Sotomayor takes the oath from Chief Justice John Roberts, right, to become the Supreme Court's first Hispanic justice and only the third woman in the Court's 220-year history, August 8, 2009. She is joined by her brother, Juan Luis Sotomayor, and her mother, Celina Sotomayor, holding the Bible. (AP Photo/J. Scott Applewhite)

In this artist rendering, the Supreme Court holds an investiture ceremony for Associate Justice Sonia Sotomayor, as Chief Justice of the United States John Roberts raises his hand to administer the judicial oath surrounded by her colleagues, and joined by President Barack Obama at lower right, and Attorney General Eric Holder, bottom. (AP Photo/Dana Verkouteren)

dard oath first in which she pledged to "support and defend the Constitution of the United States against all enemies, foreign and domestic." The group then walked to the East Conference Room for the judicial oath. There they were joined by several friends, family members as well as other supporters of Sotomayor's. As Chief Justice Roberts recited the oath, Sotomayor promised to "administer justice without respect to persons, and do equal right to the poor and to the rich, and that I will faithfully and impartially discharge and perform all the duties incumbent upon me under the Constitution and laws of the United States." Chief Justice Roberts then shook her hand, congratulated her, and welcomed her to the court, where she would begin her work as an associate justice in October. Justice Sotomayor hugged her mother and then shook hands of her well wishers.[36]

That August afternoon marked the end of a remarkable journey for Sotomayor. It began in the sprawling poverty of her mother's youth in Puerto Rico and was shaped by the determination and courage of her

*Sonia Sotomayor accompanied by Puerto Rico's Supreme Court Chief Justice
Federico Hernandez Denton, front left, and Chief U.S. District Court Judge José
Fuste, front right, in San Juan, 2009. (AP Photo/Andres Leighton)*

parents as they made a life for themselves in New York City. Her mother's strength, support, and belief in the American dream helped forge
her daughter's own dreams that moved her from the Bronxdale Houses
to Princeton, Yale Law School, and a black robe and the judge's bench.
At 55 years of age, Sonia Sotomayor was at the top of her profession
with new possibilities ahead. But this daughter of Puerto Rico, this
wise Latina, would never forget her roots. For Sonia Sotomayor, her
history and heritage were an integral part of her success: to leave those
behind would mean leaving her soul and identity behind as well. Hers
is a moving and inspiring story and will surely continue to bring hope
and the promise of a better life, success and making the world a better place, a bright beacon for those who will someday follow in her
footsteps.

NOTES

1. "Sotomayor Pledges Fidelity to the Law," *CNNPolitics*, July 13,
2009, http://articles.cnn.com/2009–07–13/politics/sotomayor.hearing_1_
supreme-court-judicial-philosophy-sonia-sotomayor?_s=PM:POLITICS.

2. Associated Press, "Sotomayor Hearings to begin July 13," *MSNBC*, June 9, 2009, http://www.msnbc.msn.com/id/31186827/ns/pol itics-supreme_court/t/sotomayor-hearings-begin-july/#.TpyHmptKO5I.

3. Ibid.

4. Ibid.

5. Lauren Collins, "Number Nine: Sonia Sotomayor's High Pro-file Debut," *New Yorker*, January 11, 2010, p. 49, Antonia Felix, *Sonia Sotomayor: The True American Dream*, New York: Berkeley Publishing Group, 2010, p. 222.

6. Tom Korologos, "The Art of Getting Confirmed," *Washington Post*, January 5, 2009, http://www.washingtonpost.com/wp-dyn/con tent/article/2009/01/04/AR2009010401437_2.html.

7. Collins, "Number Nine: Sonia Sotomayor's High Profile Debut."

8. Ibid.

9. "Sotomayor Pledges Fidelity to the Law."

10. Ari Shapiro, "Sotomayor Differs from Obama on 'Empathy' Issue," *NPR*, July 14, 2009, http://www.npr.org/templates/story/story. php?storyId=106569335&refresh=true.

11. Ibid.

12. Ibid.

13. Ibid.

14. Ibid.; Andrew Malcolm, "Sotomayor Hearings: The Judge Ex-plains the 'Wise Latina' Speech," *Los Angles Times*, July 14, 2009, http:// latimesblogs.latimes.com/washington/2009/07/sotomayor-hearings-the-judge-explains-the-wise-latina-speech.html; Warren Richey, "'Wise La-tina' a Bad Choice of Words," *Christian Science Monitor*, July 14, 2009, http://www.csmonitor.com/USA/Politics/2009/0714/sotomayor-wise-latina-a-bad-choice-of-words.

15. Shapiro, "Sotomayor Differs from Obama on 'Empathy' Issue."; Malcolm, "Sotomayor Hearings: The Judge Explains the 'Wise Latina' Speech."

16. Kate Phillips, "Live Blogging Sotomayor Hearings, Day 2," *New York Times*, July 14, 2009, http://thecaucus.blogs.nytimes.com/2009/07/14/ live-blogging-the-sotomayor-hearings-day-2/.

17. Warren Richey, "Supreme Court to Hear Reverse Discrimina-tion Case," *Christian Science Monitor*, April 22, 2009, http://www.cs monitor.com/USA/Justice/2009/0422/p03s01-usju.html.

18. Ibid.

19. Ibid.

20. Ibid.

21. Naftali Bendavid, "Firefighter Ricci Takes seat at Sotomayor Hearing," *Wall Street Journal*, July 14, 2009, http://blogs.wsj.com/wash wire/2009/07/16/firefighter-ricci-takes-witness-seat-at-sotomayor-hearing/.

22. Ibid.

23. Ibid.; Richey, "Supreme Court to Hear Reverse Discrimination Case."

24. Richey, "Supreme Court to Hear Reverse Discrimination Case;" Carol J. Williams, "Legal Experts' Views on the Sotomayor Hearings," *Los Angles Times*, July 16, 2009, http://articles.latimes.com/2009/jul/16/nation/na-sotomayor-legal16.

25. Shapiro, "Sotomayor Differs from Obama on 'Empathy' Issue."

26. "High Marks for Sotomayor After Tough Questioning," *CNNPolitics*, July 14, 2009, http://articles.cnn.com/2009–07–14/poli tics/sotomayor.hearing_1_sotomayor-hearings-wise-latina-woman-his panic-supreme-court?_s=PM:POLITICS.

27. Dana Milbank, "Firefighters, but no Brimstone," *Washington Post*, July 17, 2009, http://www.washingtonpost.com/wp-dyn/content/article/2009/07/16/AR2009071603767.html.

28. Peggy Noonan, "Sotomayor Hearing Escapes Gravity," *Wall Street Journal*, July 17, 2009 http://online.wsj.com/article/SB12477 7884829553723.html.

29. Editors, "Sotomayor Hearings a Waste of Time?," *New York Times*, July 15, 2009, http://roomfordebate.blogs.nytimes.com/2009/07/15/the-sotomayor-hearings-a-waste-of-time/.

30. Ibid.

31. Charlie Savage, "Senate Approves Sotomayor to Supreme Court," *New York Times*, August 6, 2009, http://www.nytimes.com/2009/08/07/us/politics/07confirm.html.

32. Ibid.

33. Ibid.

34. Ibid.

35. Ibid.

36. Ibid.

SELECTED BIBLIOGRAPHY

BOOKS

Felix, Antonia. *Sonia Sotomayor: The True American Dream*. New York: Berkeley Publishing Group, 2010.

Hanson, Earl Parker. *Transformation: The Story of Modern Puerto Rico*. New York: Simon & Schuster, 1955.

Marín, Luis Muñoz. "The Sad Case of Porto Rico." In *The Puerto Ricans: A Documentary History*, ed. Kal Wagenheim and Olga Jimenez de Wagenheim. New York: Markus Wiener Publishers, 1994.

Treadwell, Mattie. *The Women's Army Corps;* Washington, D.C.: Center of Military History, 1991. http://www.history.army.mil/books/wwii/wac/ch18.htm#b6.

WAC Handbook 1944. Women Veterans Historical Collection, University of North Carolina-Greensboro. http://library.uncg.edu/dp/wv/results28.aspx?i=4708&s=2.

"We Are Becoming Americanized." In *The Puerto Ricans: A Documentary History*, ed. Kal Wagenheim and Olga Jimenez de Wagenheim. New York: Markus Wiener Publishers, 1994.

ARTICLES

Associated Press. "1994 Strike as a Low Point for Baseball." *MLB-ESPN*, August 10, 2004. http://sports.espn.go.com/mlb/news/story?id=1856626.

Associated Press. "Sotomayor Hearings to Begin July 13." *MSNBC*, June 9, 2009. http://www.msnbc.msn.com/id/31186827/ns/politics-supreme_court/t/sotomayor-hearings-begin-july/#.TpyHmptKO5I.

Auerbach, Stewart. "Law Firm Apologizes to Yale Student." *Washington Post*, December 16, 1978, p. D3.

Ayala, Cèsar. "The Decline of the Plantation Economy and the Puerto Rican Migration of the 1950s." *Latino Studies Journal* 7, no. 1 (Winter 1996), p. 63–65.

Barnes, Robert. "Left and Right Begin Battle over Sotomayor's Supreme Court Nomination." *Washington Post*, May 28, 2009. http://www.washingtonpost.com/wp-dyn/content/article/2009/05/27/AR2009052703713.html?sid=ST2009052703896.

Barra, Allen. "Baseball's Costliest Walk." *Wall Street Journal*, October 28, 2009. http://online.wsj.com/article/SB10001424052748704335904574497433535880354.html.

Barzilay, Jonathan. "The D.A.'s Right Arms." *New York Times Magazine*, November 23, 1983, p. 118.

Becker, Jo and Adam Liptak. "Sotomayor's Blunt Style Raises Issue of Temperament." *New York Times*, May 28, 2009. http://www.nytimes.com/2009/05/29/us/politics/29judge.html?pagewanted=all.

Bendavid, Naftali. "Firefighter Ricci Takes Seat at Sotomayor Hearing." *Wall Street Journal*, July 14, 2009. http://blogs.wsj.com/washwire/2009/07/16/firefighter-ricci-takes-witness-seat-at-sotomayor-hearing/.

Biskupic, Joan. "Sotomayor Courtesy Calls, Not Photo ops." *USA Today*, June 18, 2009. http://www.usatoday.com/news/washington/judicial/2009–06–18-sotomayor-senate_N.htm.

Biskupic, Joan. "Sotomayor Opens Up about Her Diabetes." *USA Today*, June 24, 2011. http://www.usatoday.com/news/washington/judicial/supremecourtjustices/2011–06–21-sotomayor-diabetes-court_n.htm.

Biskupic, Joan and Kathy Kiely. "Perry Masons' Stories 'Molded' Sotomayor." *USA Today*, July 23, 2009. http://www.usatoday.com/news/washington/judicial/2009–07–15-sotomayor-video-hearing_N.htm.

Bort, Ina R. "Judicial Profile: Hon. Sonia Sotomayor." *The Federal Lawyer* 53, no. 2 (February 2006), p. 37.

Brenner, Elsa. "Everything You Need in One Giant Package." *New York Times*, April 6, 2008. http://www.nytimes.com/2008/04/06/realestate/06live.html.

Collins, Lauren. "Number Nine: Sonia Sotomayor's High Profile Debut." *The New Yorker*, January 11, 2010, pp. 42–55.

Debendetti, Gabriel. "At Princeton, Sotomayor '76 Excelled at Academics, Extracurriculars." *The Daily Princetonian*, May 13, 2009. http://www.dailyprincetonian.com/2009/05/13/23695/.

"Did Sotomayor Save Baseball?" *The Economist*, May 27, 2009. http://www.economist.com/blogs/democracyinamerica/2009/05/did_sotomayor_save_baseball.

"District Attorney of New York County Robert Morgenthau Testifies at Judge Sotomayor's Confirmation Hearings." *Washington Post*, July 16, 2009. http://www.washingtonpost.com/wp-dyn/content/article/2009/07/16/AR2009071602990.html.

Donnally, Trish. "Fashion's Assault on Counterfeiters; Companies Fight to Stop Others Cashing in on Their Good Name." *The San Francisco Chronicle*, May 20, 1992, p. D3.

Epstein, Richard A. "The Sotomayor Nomination." *Forbes*, May 26, 2009. http://www.forbes.com/2009/05/26/supreme-court-nomination-obama-opinions-columnists-sonia-sotomayor.html.

Fernandez, Manny. "The Children at the Judge's Bronx School." *New York Times*, July 15, 2009. http://www.nytimes.com/2009/07/16/nyregion/16bronx.html?ref=nyregion.

Gregory, Sean. "How Sotomayor 'Saved' Baseball." *Time*, May 26, 2009. http://www.time.com/time/nation/article/0,8599,1900974,00.html.

Gross, Michael. "Fashion Notes." *New York Times*, November 11, 1986, A16.

Hoffman, Jan. "A Breakthrough Judge: What She Always Wanted." *New York Times*, September 25, 1992, B16.

Hoffman, Jan. "Nancy Drew's Granddaughters." *New York Times*, July 17, 2009. http://www.nytimes.com/2009/07/19/fashion/19drew.html? pagewanted=all.

Horowitz, Jason. "The Many Rabbis of Sonia Sotomayor." *New York Observers Politicker NY*, May 26, 2009. http://www.observer. com/3719/many-rabbis-sonia-sotomayor.

"Induction Proceedings for Judge Sonia Sotomayor, November 6, 1998, United States Court House, 500 Pearl Street, New York, NY."

Kelliman, Laurie. "Sotomayor Speeches Detail Life, Uncertainties." *Salt Lake Tribune*, June 5, 2009. http://archive.sltrib.com/article. php?id=12527117&itype=NGPSID&keyword=&qtype=.

Kiely, Kathy. "No Dissent: A Locomotive for Sotomayor '76." June 1, 2011. http://paw.princeton.edu/issues/2011/06/01/pages/4772/index. xml.

King, Wayne. "Now, No Hispanic Candidates for Federal Bench in New York." *The New York Times*, February 15, 1991. http://www. nytimes.com/1991/02/15/nyregion/now-no-hispanic-candidates- for-federal-bench-in-new-york.html?src=pm.

Kolker, Robert. "Happy 85th Birthday Bob Morgenthau." *New York Magazine*, May 25, 2005. http://nymag.com/nymetro/news/poli tics/newyork/features/9546/.

Landau, Elizabeth. "Cricket, Ivy League Classmates Startled Student Sonia Sotomayor." *CNN*, July 15, 2009. http://articles.cnn. com/2009–07–15/us/sotomayor.college_1_cricket-sonia-soto mayor-classmates?_s=PM:US.

Landau, Elizabeth. "Sotomayor Always Willing to Speak Up at Yale Law." *CNNPolitics*, May 26, 2009. http://articles.cnn.com/2009– 05–26/politics/sotomayor.princeton.yale_1_yale-law-school- classmates-sonia-sotomayor?_s=PM:POLITICS.

Lawton, Catherine. "A Touch of Class." *Mademoiselle*, September 1986.

Lewis, Neil A. "G.O.P., Its Eyes on High Court, Blocks a Judge." *New York Times*, June 13, 1998, A1.

Lewis, Neil A. "On a Supreme Court Prospect's Resume: 'Baseball Savior,'" *New York Times*, May 14, 2009. http://www.nytimes. com/2009/05/15/us/15sotomayor.html?ref=soniasotomayor.

Lipke, David. "Judge Sotomayor's Fashionable Past (Sonia Sotomayor)." *Women's Wear Daily*, July 1, 2009. http://www.accessmylibrary.

com/article-1G1–203645860/judge-sotomayor-fashionable-past. html.

Lucas, Lisa and David Saltonstall. "Sonia Sotomayor's Mother Tells News: I Overcame Odds to Raise U.S. Supreme Court Pick." *New York Daily News*, May 27, 2009. http://articles.nydaily news.com/2009–05–27/news/17922654_1_celina-sotomayor-supreme-court-sonia-sotomayor.

Mai-Duc, Christine. "Sonia Sotomayor Discusses Her Diabetes with Children's Group." *Los Angeles Times*, June 21, 2011. http://www. latimes.com/health/la-na-sotomayor-diabetes-20110622, 0,6515717.story.

Malcolm, Andrew. "Sotomayor Hearings: The Judge Explains the 'Wise Latina' Speech." *Los Angles Times*, July 14, 2009. http://latimes blogs.latimes.com/washington/2009/07/sotomayor-hearings-the-judge-explains-the-wise-latina-speech.html.

McKinnon, John D. "Sotomayor: Fighting for . . . Fendi?." *Wall Street Journal*, May 26, 2009. http://blogs.wsj.com/washwire/2009/05/26/ sotomayor-fighting-forfendi/.

Milbank, Dana. "Firefighters, but no Brimstone." *Washington Post*, July 17, 2009. http://www.washingtonpost.com/wp-dyn/content/article/ 2009/07/16/AR2009071603767.html.

Miller, Zeke. "At Yale Sotomayor was Sharp but Not Outspoken." *Yale Daily News*, May 31, 2009. http://www.yaledailynews.com/ news/2009/may/31/at-yale-sotomayor-was-sharp-but-not-out spoken/.

Miranda, Carolina A. "Just What is a 'Wise Latina' Anyway?" *Time*, July 14, 2009. http://www.time.com/time/politics/article/0,8599, 1910403,00.html.

Neil, Martha. "Fendi Crush was Highlight of Sotomayor's IP Practice." *ABA Journal*, May 26, 2009. http://www.abajournal.com/news/ article/fendi_crush_was_highlight_of_sotomayors_ip_practice.

Noonan, Peggy. "Sotomayor Hearing Escapes Gravity." *Wall Street Journal*, July 17, 2009. http://online.wsj.com/article/SB124777884829553723. html.

Oliphant, James. "Sotomayor Remembered as Zealous Prosecutor." *Los Angeles Times*, June 9, 2009. http://articles.latimes.com/2009/ jun/09/nation/na-sotomayor-prosecutor9.

Oliphant, James and Andrew Zajac. "At Yale, Sotomayor Won Apology from Law Firm." May 29, 2009, *Los Angeles Times*. http://articles.latimes.com/2009/may/28/nation/na-sotomayor-apology28.

Pico, Fernando. "Let Puerto Rico Decide." *America*, May 30, 1998: 3+. *Expanded Academic ASAP*. Web. 30 July 2011. .http://find.galegroup.com/gps/infomark.do?&contentSet=IAC-Documents&type=retrieve&tabID=T003&prodId=IPS&docId=A20748211&source=gale&srcprod=EAIM&userGroupName=ches75568&version=1.0.

Powell, Michael. "To Get to Sotomayor's Core, Go to New York." *The New York Times*, July 9, 2009. http://www.nytimes.com/2009/07/10/nyregion/10sonia.html?pagewanted=all.

Powell, Michael and Serge Kovaleski. "Sotomayor Rose on Merit Alone, Her Allies Say." *New York Times*, June 4, 2009. http://www.nytimes.com/2009/06/05/us/politics/05judge.html.

Richey, Warren. "Supreme Court to Hear Reverse Discrimination Case." *Christian Science Monitor*, April 22, 2009. http://www.csmonitor.com/USA/Justice/2009/0422/p03s01-usju.html.

Savage, Charlie. "Senate Approves Sotomayor to Supreme Court." *The New York Times*, August 6, 2009. http://www.nytimes.com/2009/08/07/us/politics/07confirm.html.

Savage, Charlie. "Sotomayor Sworn in as Supreme Court Justice." *The New York Times*, August 6, 2009. http://www.nytimes.com/2009/08/09/us/politics/09sotomayor.html.

Savage, Charlie and Michael Powell. "Sotomayor Put Focus on the Poor." *New York Times*, June 18, 2009. http://www.tmg-housing.com/PDF/Sotomayor.pdf.

"Senators Say Sotomayor Impressive in Meetings." *USA Today*, June 14, 2009. http://www.usatoday.com/news/washington/2009-06-13-sotomayor-interviews_N.htm.

Shapiro, Ari. "Sotomayor Differs from Obama on 'Empathy' Issue." *NPR*, July 14, 2009. http://www.npr.org/templates/story/story.php?storyId=106569335&refresh=true.

Shapiro, Walter, John Dickerson, Janet I-Chin, and David S. Jackson. "Bummer of '94." *Time*, August 22, 1994. http://www.time.com/time/magazine/article/0,9171,981283,00.html.

Shulman, Robin. "Sonia Sotomayor Built Successful Life on Then-Solid Ground of Bronxdale Houses." *Washington Post*, June 16, 2009. http://www.washingtonpost.com/wp-dyn/content/article/2009/06/15/AR2009061503170.html.

Sloan, Karen. "Sotomayor's Civil Practice was with a Small, but Specialized Firm." *The National Law Journal*, May 28, 2009. http://www.law.com/jsp/nlj/PubArticleNLJ.jsp?id=1202431049336.

Smith, Greg B., "Judges Journey to Top Bronx' Sotomayor Rose from Projects to Court of Appeals." *Daily News*, October 24, 1998, p. 17.

Sotomayor, Sonia. "A Latina Judge's Voice." *New York Times*, May 14, 2009. http://www.nytimes.com/2009/05/15/us/politics/15judge.text.html?pagewanted=all.

"Sotomayor Confirmation Hearings Day 2." *The New York Times*, July 14, 2009. http://www.nytimes.com/2009/07/14/us/politics/14confirm-text.html?pagewanted=all.

"Sotomayor Hearings a Waste of Time?" *New York Times*, July 15, 2009. http://roomfordebate.blogs.nytimes.com/2009/07/15/the-sotomayor-hearings-a-waste-of-time/.

Stephens, Joe and Del Quentin Wilber. "Gritty First Job Shaped Nominee." *The Washington Post*, June 4, 2009, p. A01.

Stolberg, Sheryl Gay. "Court Nominee Manages Diabetes with Discipline." *New York Times*, July 9, 2009. http://www.nytimes.com/2009/07/10/us/politics/10diabetes.html.

Stolberg, Sheryl Gay. "A Trailblazer and a Dreamer," *New York Times* 27 May 2009: A1(L).

Tedford, Deborah. "Obama Chooses Sotomayor for High Court." *NPR*, May 26, 2009. http://www.npr.org/templates/story/story.php?storyId=104530389.

Temple-Raston, Dina. "Sotomayor's Real-World Schooling in Law and Order." *NPR*. http://www.npr.org/templates/story/story.php?storyId=105005007.

Thomas, Dana. "The Cost of Counterfeiting." *Lo$t*, December 2008–January 2009. http://www.lostmag.com/issue29/counterfeiting.php.

Thomas, Evan, Stuart Taylor Jr., and Brian No. "Meet the Sotomayors." *Newsweek*, July 20, 2009, p. 43.

Tomlinson, Brett. "Sotomayor in PAW." *Princeton Alumni Weekly*, July 13, 2009. http://blogs.princeton.edu/paw/2009/07/sotomayor_in_pa.html.

Totenberg, Nina. "How Obama's Nomination of Sotomayor Unfolded." *NPR*, May 28, 2009. http://www.npr.org/templates/story/story.php?storyId=104648062.

Vecsey, George. "Hope Comes to Baseball Just in Time." *New York Times*, April 1, 1995, p. 29.

Weister, Benjamin and William K. Rashbaum. "Sotomayor is Recalled as a Driven Rookie Prosecutor." *The New York Times*, June 8, 2009, Section A, p. 13.

Westfall, Sandra Sobieraj. "Sonia Sotomayor: From the Bronx to the Bench." *People*, August 17, 2009, p. 75.

Williams, Carol J. "Legal Experts' Views on the Sotomayor Hearings." *Los Angles Times*, July 16, 2009. http://articles.latimes.com/2009/jul/16/nation/na-sotomayor-legal16.

Winn, Peter. "Mentor at Princeton Recalls Sotomayor's Evolution." *The Washington Post*, July 12, 2009. http://www.washingtonpost.com/wp-dyn/content/article/2009/07/09/AR2009070902391.html.

WEBSITES

"Bronxdale Houses." http://www.nyc.gov/html/nycha/html/developments/bronxdalehouses.shtml.

"Confirmation Hearing on Hon. Susan Black, Sonia Sotomayor, Loretta Preska and Irene M. Keeley, U.S. Senate Committee on the Judiciary, June 4, 1991." http://www.scotusblog.com/wp-content/uploads/2009/06/sotomayor-district-hearing.pdf.

Dengler, Charisse. "Linda Fairstein: Author and Former Head of the Manhattan District Attorney's Office's Sex Crimes Unit." *LawCrossing*. http://www.lawcrossing.com/article/2403/Linda-Fairstein-Author-and-Former-Head-of-the-Manhattan-District-Attorney-s-Office-s-Sex-Crimes-Unit/.

EconomyWatch. "History of Mergers and Acquisitions." http://www.economywatch.com/mergers-acquisitions/history.html.

Ferreira, Jason Michael. "Student Movements—New Student Organizations, Continuing Organization, New York Times, Educational Opportunity Program, Puerto Ricans for Educational Progress." http://www.jrank.org/cultures/pages/4473/Student-Movements. html.

"Hearings Before The Committee on the Judiciary, United States Senate, September 5, 30, October 28, 29, November 12, 1997." http://www.archive.org/stream/confirmationhear972unit/confir mationhear972unit_djvu.txt.

"High Marks for Sotomayor after tough questioning." *CNNPolitics,* July 14, 2009. http://articles.cnn.com/2009–07–14/politics/so tomayor.hearing_1_sotomayor-hearings-wise-latina-woman-his panic-supreme-court?_s=PM:POLITICS.

"The History of Fendi." http://www.fendi.com/#/en/foreverfendi/histo ryoffendi.

"History of YLS." http://www.law.yale.edu/about/historyofyls.htm#.

Lajas, Puerto Rico." http://www.lajaspr.com/engHistoriaLlama.htm.

Mears, Bill. "Analysis: Obama's first judicial pick signals fight for control." *CNNPolitics,* March 18, 2009. http://www.cnn.com/2009/ POLITICS/03/18/obama.judiciary/index.html?iref=allsearch.

Mears, Bill. "Sotomayor says she was the 'perfect affirmative action baby.'"*CNNPolitics,* June 11, 2009. http://articles.cnn.com/2009–06–11/politics/sotomayor.affirmative.action_1_affirmative-ac tion-wise-latina-woman-test-scores?_s=PM:POLITICS.

Meany, Joseph F. Jr. "Port in a Storm: The Port of New York in World War II." New York State Museum. http://www.nysm.nysed.gov/ research_collections/research/history/hisportofnewyork.html.

Miller, Carlin DeGuerin. "Real Life 'Law & Order' DA Robert Morgenthau Retires at 90." *CBS News,* December 31, 2009. http:// www.cbsnews.com/8301–504083_162–6041975–504083.html.

"New York Crime Rates 1960–2009." http://www.disastercenter.com/ crime/nycrime.htm.

"*New York v. Ferber*: Significance." *LawJrank.* http://law.jrank.org/ pages/23393/New-York-v-Ferber-Significance.html.

"Obama's Sotomayor Nomination Remarks." MSNBC *White House,* May 26, 2009. http://www.msnbc.msn.com/id/30943237/ns/pol

itics-white_house/t/obamas-sotomayor-nomination-remarks/#. TptFrZtKO5I.

OCED. "The Economic Impact of Counterfeiting." http://www.oecd. org/dataoecd/11/11/2090589.pdf.

Pavia & Harcourt. "Our Profile." http://www.pavialaw.com/profile.cfm.

"Puerto Rican Emigration: Why the 1950s?" http://lcw.lehman.edu/ lehman/depts/latinampuertorican/latinoweb/PuertoRico/1950s. htm.

Phillips, Kate. "Live Blogging Sotomayor Hearings, Day 2." *The New York Times*, July 14, 2009. http://thecaucus.blogs.nytimes. com/2009/07/14/live-blogging-the-sotomayor-hearings-day-2/.

Princeton University. "Princeton University at a Glance." http://www. princeton.edu/main/about/history/glance/.

"Quotes." Baker Hostetler, July 13, 2010. http://www.bakerlaw.com/ar- ticles/sonia-sotomayor-the-true-american-dream-07–13–2010/.

Rodriguez, Clara E. "Puerto Ricans: Immigrants and Migrants: A Historical Perspective." AmericansAll, A National Education Program. http://www.americansall.com/PDFs/02-americans-all/ 9.9.pdf.

"Second Circuit Court." Federal Judicial Center. http://www.fjc.gov/ history/home.nsf/page/courts_of_appeals.html.

"Senate Questionnaire Details Sotomayor's Interviews." *The BLT: The Blog of LegalTimes*, June 4, 2009. http://legaltimes.typepad.com/ blt/2009/06/sotomayor-submits-questionnaire-to-senate-judi ciary.html.

Sotomayor, Sonia. "Pace Law School Honorary Degree Acceptance Speech." May 18, 2003. http://www.law.pace.edu/files/com mencement/honorarydegree/SotomayorSpeech05182003.pdf.

Sotomayor, Sonia. "Remarks Prepared for Delivery at the Lehman Col- lege Commencement." June 3, 1999. http://www.lehman.cuny. edu/lehman/enews/2009_05_18/pdf/sotomayor_remarks.pdf.

"Sotomayor Pledges Fidelity to the Law." *CNNPolitics*, July 13, 2009. http://articles.cnn.com/2009–07–13/politics/sotomayor.hear ing_1_supreme-court-judicial-philosophy-sonia-sotomayor?_ s=PM:POLITICS.

"Soundview, Bronx." http://en.wikipedia.org/wiki/Soundview,_Bronx.

"Testimony of Theodore Shaw, July 16, 2009." http://judiciary.senate. gov/hearings/testimony.cfm?id=e655f9e2809e5476862f735da14 d3b3b&wit_id=e655f9e2809e5476862f735da14d3b3b-4–3.

White, Byron. "Opinion of the Court, Supreme Court of the United States, 458 U.S. 747, *New York v. Ferber*." http://www.law.cornell. edu/supct/html/historics/USSC_CR_0458_0747_ZO.html.

COURT CASES

Campos v. Coughlin (1994)

Silverman v. Major League Baseball Player Relations Committee (1995)

Gant v. Wallingford Board of Education (1999)

N.G. & S.G. ex rel. S.C. v. Connecticut (2004)

U.S. v. Falso (2008)

Ricci v. DeStefano (2008)

INDEX